Transforming High Schools through Response to Intervention (RtI)

Lessons Learned and a Pathway Forward

Jeremy Koselak

Eye On Education
6 Depot Way West, Suite 106
Larchmont, NY 10538
(914) 833-0551
(914) 833-0761 fax
www.eyeoneducation.com

For information about permission to reproduce selections from this book,
write: Eye On Education, Permissions Dept., Suite 106, 6 Depot Way West,
Larchmont, NY 10538

Library of Congress Cataloging-in-Publication Data

Koselak, Jeremy.
Transforming high schools through response to intervention (RTI) : lessons
learned and a pathway forward/by Jeremy Koselak.
    p.   cm.
Includes bibliographical references.
 ISBN 978-1-59667-177-5
1. Reading—Remedial teaching.
2. Reading (Middle school)
3. Reading (Secondary)
4. Response to intervention (Learning disabled children)
I. Title.
LB1050.5.K585 2011
372.43--dc22   2010053323

10 9 8 7 6 5 4 3 2 1

Also Available from EYE ON EDUCATION

Response to Intervention and Continuous School Improvement:
Using Data, Vision, and Leadership to Design, Implement,
and Evaluate a Schoolwide Prevention System
Victoria L. Bernhardt and Connie L. Hebert

Questions and Answers About RTI:
A Guide to Success
Heather Moran and Anthony Petruzzelli

RTI Strategies that Work in the K-2 Classroom
Eli Johnson and Michelle Karns

I Have the Data . . . Now What?
Analyzing Data and Making Instructional Changes
Betsy Moore

Rigorous Schools and Classrooms:
Leading the Way
Ronald Williamson and Barbara R. Blackburn

Leading School Change:
9 Strategies to Bring Everybody On Board
Todd Whitaker

Student Achievement Goal Setting:
Using Data to Improve Teaching and Learning
James H. Stronge and Leslie W. Grant

Using Data to Improve Student Learning in High Schools
Victoria L. Bernhardt

Data-Driven Decision Making and Dynamic Planning:
A School Leader's Guide
Paul G. Preuss

Teaching, Learning, and Assessment Together:
Reflective Assessments for Middle and High School
English and Social Studies
Arthur K. Ellis and Laurynn Evans

Teaching, Learning, and Assessment Together:
Reflective Assessments for Middle and High School
Mathematics and Science
Arthur K. Ellis and David W. Denton

Table of Contents

Free Downloads

Selected figures displayed in this book are available on Eye On Education's website as Adobe Acrobat files. Permission has been granted to purchasers of this book to download and print these figures.

You can access these downloads by visiting Eye On Education's website: www.eyeoneducation.com. Click FREE Downloads. You can also search or browse our website for this book, and then log in to access the downloads.

You'll need your bookbuyer access code: **HSRTI-7177-5**

Bonus! The following downloads extend and expand the material in the book and are available to bookbuyers on our website.

Peer Coach Training Guide
Peer Coach Evaluation Rubric
Schoolwide Tiered Intervention Schedule

Acknowledgments

Karen Littlejohn for tireless efforts to make the SSC work so well and for her incredible work with struggling students

Brooke Bell for helping to guide our school's RtI process from a special education mandate into a schoolwide priority

Leah Bitat for honest discussions about the difficulties of RtI and SLD

Leslie Wolken for being a significant contributor to the development of the SSC

Tom Kelly for exceptional administrative support and trust in the development of the SSC

Dave Sawtelle, Paul Hartman, Cindy Aguilar, John Krakauer, and Jeremy Joiner for pushing to improve alignment and implement standards-based grading practices

Patty Lavandar for focused data work and support

Lara Disney for leadership and collaboration

Bryan Adler for guidance with data

Shana Frederick for guidance on SLD

Mel Bethards for efforts on the PST

Robert Sickles and Jennifer Lee for commitment, support and patience in the building of this book

Family!—who made many sacrifices so I could have time to research and write this book: Laura Koselak, Jacob and Mitchell Warmingham, Cassian and Kaden, Lisa Koselak, Kaye and Mike Brabec, David Brabec, and Jenny Hall. I am grateful for the encouragement I received from all my siblings (especially Laina, Heather, and Josh), who claimed I would be a writer before I ever believed it.

About the Author

The author has worked for eleven years with at-risk high school students across all content areas, in a variety of settings, with a focus on mathematics. Recognized in 2003 as Teacher of the Year by the Colorado Association of Family and Children Agencies, he has dedicated his career to working with students who struggle in high school. He has two bachelor's degrees (in economics and history) and a master's degree in special education. He is currently the RtI coordinator and director of the Student Support Center at an urban high school in Colorado Springs.

Introduction

Why RtI?

Response to Intervention (RtI) is a framework of tiered instruction designed to improve learning outcomes for all students. Driven by data-based decision-making, it is a systemic, efficient, timely, and dynamic way to help all students. When properly implemented, RtI also ensures delivery of research-based instruction and fidelity of interventions. Furthermore, RtI is anticipated by many educators to be the key to school reform. It is filled with potential and hope. The expanding body of research literature identifies the following results:

1. RtI strengthens schools' overall performance (Shannon, 2007).
2. RtI improves learning outcomes for struggling learners (Mellard, Byrd, Johnson, Tollefson, & Boesche, 2004).
3. RtI reduces the number of students incorrectly labeled with a learning disability (false positives) because of cultural differences or poor instruction (Cortiella, 2005; O'Connor, Harty, & Fulmer 2005; Speece, Case, & Molloy, 2003).

Why This Book?

As our high school RtI team struggled six years ago to find advice in the research literature and training, we discovered an inadequate set of guidelines and practical implementation models to follow. We therefore created a version of secondary school RtI that worked well in our setting and have shared this process with other schools around the country. Currently, and certainly to the benefit of schools new to RtI, the literature and research are beginning to emerge. This book complements and synthesizes the emerging research and presents a specific approach that takes into account the unique challenges high schools face regarding RtI.

Though a one-size-fits-all RtI model is not realistic (nor necessarily desirable), this book looks to outline a concise pathway that avoids common pitfalls and highlights essential elements for RtI implementation. One such element that our school has developed, a student support center, has been instrumental in our ability to flexibly and strategically deliver interventions at the high school level. An additional goal of this book is to highlight the features of RtI worth implementing now while also bringing attention to the features of RtI that demand further research prior to initiation.

Structure of the Book

Thematically, this book covers the following concepts:

◆ Hope
◆ Principle elements and research
◆ Challenges for high schools, including limitations for special education eligibility determination
◆ Implementation pathway
  • Study, plan, sustain, and share RtI implementation
  • Embed data-based decision-making across all systems and tiers
  • Establish a tiered model of instruction and intervention

The threads running throughout the book will be

◆ the use of data-based decision-making (DBDM) in guiding response to instruction and intervention
◆ lessons learned
◆ templates, figures, and graphs to demonstrate actual high school samples
◆ reflections, case studies, and examples for high school settings

The book also includes a glossary, a diverse Resources section for practitioners, and extensive appendices containing forms and further RtI resources.

Throughout the book, I will argue that schools must make two careful distinctions as they differentiate the purpose of RtI and its role in special education.

1. Schools should differentiate the roles of the RtI leadership team and the problem-solving team. While both teams must use data-based decision-making, the RTI leadership team handles planning, systemic implementation, and ongoing evaluation of academic and behavior tiered structures. The problem-solving team (PST) focuses on individual student learning plans and responsiveness to targeted interventions.

2. RtI's best features (those backed by research) should be highlighted while its more contentious and ambiguous elements should be curtailed until more research surfaces. The core elements that establish RtI as a premium framework for early, preventive support for struggling students are widely supported in the research literature and are practically sound. The ambiguity enters the discussion when schools consider using RtI to determine specific learning disability (SLD) eligibility or to consistently determine what constitutes adequate response to intervention at various tiers, including clear decision rules validated in the research.

While implementers of RtI can be assured that the basic tenets are sound, practical, research-based, and clear, they should also be aware that the applicability of this framework to the determination of SLD is far from clear or reliable and remains in contention. Not all researchers agree that even a well-articulated RtI process (like the ones in Minnesota and Colorado) should be the primary means to diagnose a learning disability. Though this book will not dedicate much space to the role of RtI as it relates to special education determination, the topic does come up at various points and Colorado's model will receive some attention in Chapter 3 (also in various appendices).

Based on the impact it has had in our building and in other schools across the country, RtI has much to offer as a general education initiative. For the sake of creating a school climate that is relentlessly focused on improving learning outcomes for *all* students, I would challenge readers to approach RtI first and foremost as a general education initiative (Response to *Instruction*), not as the primary assessment construct for special education entitlement.

1

A Story of Hope: How RtI Transformed Our High School

Though challenging, RtI has great potential to transform high schools across the nation. With talk of school reform and accountability on the rise, RtI offers promise as a framework for organizing schools and aligning systems to achieve measurable results. It is not a program but rather an approach to reaching all students more effectively through tiered supports, a focus on research-based instruction and intervention, and data-based decision-making. RtI is school reform that has the potential to improve outcomes for general education, interventions, and special education.

High-Performing School with Changing Demographics

The high school discussed in this book is an urban high school in Colorado Springs, Colorado (1,850 average student enrollment, 32% minority, 34% free or reduced lunch). Ranked in the top 1,500 nationally for four years running, it is one of five high schools in a large Colorado school district (29,000 students, 39% minority, 51% free or reduced lunch). The state of Colorado has been a pioneer in RtI implementation. While the state has been at the forefront, and the district has been leading the way in the state, our high school has been recognized as an exemplar in the district and has hosted visitors from schools all over the United States (and Australia).

FIGURE 1.1 Credit Proficiency After the First High School Semester

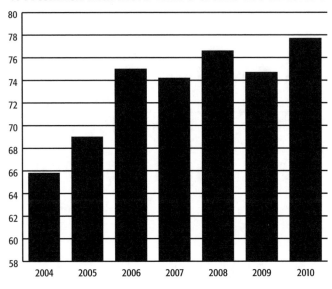

% Freshmen with More Than 5 credits at Semester 1

Our school has grown into this model gradually, achieving notable and encouraging results. In the years before the onset of RtI, our graduation rates consistently hovered below the state average, though we have been considered a high-performing school with an excellent track record with students in the Advanced Placement and International Baccalaureate Programmes. However, we were not effectively meeting the needs of our changing demographics: more at-risk students. To be proactive, we implemented RtI with an initial and intense focus on freshmen credit proficiency for the first semester. Believing that starting out on the right foot is essential, we invested heavily into freshmen success, especially in English and Math, areas in which we have seen incredible success because of RtI. Figure 1.1 demonstrates the impact of this targeted focus.

A few statistics stand out. In the two years prior to RtI implementation (2004-2005), an average of 67.4% of our freshmen were earning enough credits during the first semester (more than five) to be considered "credit proficient." In the years with RtI and Professional Learning Communities in place, our freshmen credit proficiency rate has increased to an average of 75.6%, topping off this last year at 77.7%, our highest rate on record. Furthermore, in the years we have benefited from our most dynamic intervention, the Student Support Center (2008-2010), our freshmen credit proficiency rate is averaging 76.3%. In terms of actual student numbers, about 39 more students, on

FIGURE 1.2 Graduation Rates in Colorado and Our High School

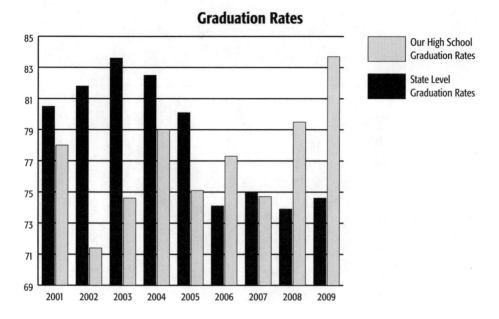

average, are credit-proficient after the first high school semester with RtI in place (including PLCs and our Student Support Center).

Given this success with freshmen at the beginning of their high school experience, we expected (and continue to expect) to see our graduation rates improve in subsequent years. Figure 1.2 demonstrates this positive and significant jump in graduation rates in 2008 and 2009 and compares them to the state graduation rates. Our highest graduation rate of recent record occurred in 2009, coinciding with our ramping up of RtI across all grade levels.

RtI's validity is to be measured by outcomes (Batsche et al., 2006), and graduation must be one key measure for high schools. The data in Figure 1.1 and 1.2 are cause for celebration for our high school, especially considering that the percentage of students receiving free and reduced lunch continues to increase steadily, from 20% in 2002 to 34% in 2009. In fact, the changing demographics motivated our movement toward a more sensitive, tiered approach to assist struggling students. The percentage of graduating students is an important measure, but it does not necessarily speak expressly to the topic of student learning. This may be measured by different metrics, but in our state, *all* juniors must take the ACT exam. On this national exam, our school has consistently outperformed the state averages. Because *all* students, not just college-bound students, must take the exam in Colorado, the comparison to national averages is not meaningful, except to note that the data over the five-year trend have been very flat for all score categories (see ACT web page

FIGURE 1.3 ACT Data for Our High School

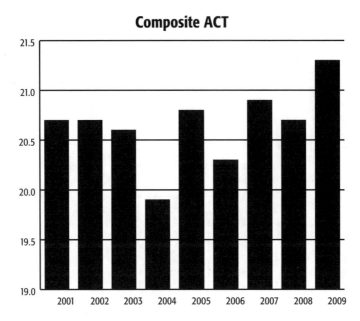

Composite ACT

in Resources section). Figure 1.3 illustrates the trend of our ACT composite score over the past seven years.

If RtI were to have a similar impact upon ACT scores as it did upon graduation rates, we would hope to see an increase in scores by 2007 (because juniors take the test). Indeed, our highest three-year composite average occurred during the years 2007 through 2009 compared to all previous years. In fact, 2009 represented our highest composite average yet, 21.3.

Since, as noted previously, our free and reduced lunch population continues to increase (correspondingly our risk factors for school struggle are increasing), the data showing improvement in our ACT scores and graduation rates seem all the more encouraging. More students (of all backgrounds and risk factors) are graduating from our school *and* they are performing better on the national exam. Evidence suggests that RtI has been a central cause of the transformation.

Beyond the quantitative data sets, RtI has also had a qualitative impact upon students, teachers and staff, administration, and parents. We have become more student-focused, flexible, responsive, collaborative, results-oriented, and accountable to our community. Above all, RtI enables high schools to reach *all* students more effectively. The sooner schools accept that RtI must be framed as a general education priority, the sooner the implementation can deliver transformation.

The following lists, though not exhaustive, suggest some of the benefits RtI offers to students, staff, administrators, and parents. Many of these benefits are drawn from our own experience and are also validated in the research literature (see Chapter 2 and the Resources section for more details on the research that supports RtI).

Benefits for Students

- ♦ Ensures that quality instruction is provided in the classroom
- ♦ Meets students where they are and helps them make progress toward goals
- ♦ Provides frequent and specific feedback about progress toward goals
- ♦ Provides layers of support to students before and as a problem develops and wraps support around them without the necessity of a disability label
- ♦ Promotes flexibility and adjusts support based on how a student responds to an intervention
- ♦ Provides opportunities for students to have input into decisions regarding intervention selection (thus increasing commitment and ownership)
- ♦ Encourages students to self-monitor data and take an active role in instruction, fostering independence and intrinsic motivation
- ♦ Customizes interventions based on specific student needs and provides more choices
- ♦ Allows for multiple ways and opportunities for students to demonstrate progress and achievement rather than a singular, point-in-time, aptitude test
- ♦ Increases likelihood of passing classes and graduating
- ♦ Enhances likelihood of improving academic skills as measured by standardized test performance
- ♦ Offers individualized attention from a team of education professionals who are vested in student success

Benefits for Teachers and Staff

- ♦ Makes the task of monitoring students' learning more efficient
- ♦ Allows teachers to identify and reach struggling students quickly and accurately
- ♦ Promotes more meaningful and cohesive professional development
- ♦ Identifies areas of concern for struggling learners efficiently and rapidly

- ◆ Improves relevance of grading and student feedback
- ◆ Alleviates overcrowding of intervention classes (dumping)
- ◆ Collaboratively brings special educators, interventionists, and general educators together to focus on "all our students"
- ◆ Increases diversity of teachers incorporated into the decision-making process
- ◆ Improvement of curriculum and instruction are built into practice and valued (time is allocated and valued for data-driven professional development and professional learning communities)

Benefits for Administrators

- ◆ Raises schoolwide expectations and increases accountability
- ◆ Clarifies and aligns the school's vision upon measurable outcomes
- ◆ Organizes intervention offerings to ensure increased efficiency
- ◆ Streamlines professional development
- ◆ Emphasizes a culture of helping *all* students
- ◆ Increases transparency of curriculum and instruction
- ◆ Installs continuous improvement as the goal of all systems
- ◆ Ensures data drives decision-making
- ◆ Builds flexibility and creativity into the routine (RtI is not a one-size-fits-all program)

Benefits for Parents

- ◆ Provides transparency of curriculum, instruction, and intervention
- ◆ Involves parents in problem-solving process before any special education labeling
- ◆ Provides relevant and timely feedback about students' progress
- ◆ Provides layers of support to help students reach goals without any need for special education label
- ◆ Ensures that quality instruction is implemented with fidelity and research-based practices are in place for students

In our school and beyond, RtI has demonstrated incredible potential to move schools in a positive direction when implemented effectively. Indeed, more and more research institutions are singing RtI's praises and making recommendations regarding its key components (as the next chapter will illustrate).

It is also true that RtI will provide endless challenges along the pathway of implementation. Wherever your school (district or state) is upon this journey, keep in mind that the benefits offered across the school setting will be well worth the effort.

The challenge for high schools is to call attention to the benefits of RtI while distancing themselves from the contentious elements (the use of RtI for SLD diagnosis) that still lack consistent backing by empirical research. The remainder of this book will crystallize both sets of features: those we should build now, and those that demand we wait.

2

Core Elements for Establishing an RtI Framework in High Schools

Response to Intervention is a cohesive framework that offers a structure for solving problems and improving outcomes, from large-scale, district- and state-level change to individualized, student-level concerns (Batsche et al., 2006). RtI pedagogy advocates that we provide tiered supports (interventions) to best help all students and use data-based decision-making (DBDM) to evaluate the effectiveness of the entire process. It is a student-centered model that looks to help students first instead of hastily labeling them with a disability. It offers a diverse set of protocols that expands the medical model (Caplan, 1964) of assessment and treatment to educational practices. On the surface, RtI offers a simple and logical approach to improve student learning.

So, beyond the definition, what is RtI's ultimate purpose for high schools? How do we know if a high school is "doing" RtI? What groups sanction it as a means to help schools and is there research to support the claims? Why is it so difficult (for high schools in particular)? What elements of a school's culture will increase the likelihood of RtI's success? The following statements will, I hope, provide answers to these questions and several more.

RtI is widely supported by a growing group of education professionals and organizations.

RtI has been recommended as a promising means of preventive and early intervention for struggling learners by many professional organizations (see Resources section for this list, which continues to expand). From the general classroom to special education services, RtI is spreading quickly as a means of ensuring that quality instruction, curriculum, and interventions are provided to all students. Dozens of national and state-level RtI websites, research centers, and books promote various training modules and resources to help districts with implementation (see Resources section). Education conferences and professional development are increasingly focused on the specifics of RtI. No matter what school, what district, or what state you are working in, it is highly likely the term "RtI" has become ubiquitous.

Although there is a more robust literature basis for RtI at the elementary level, an emerging body of evidence documents RtI's effectiveness beyond reading and elementary grade level (Mellard, 2004; Berkeley, Bender, Peaster, & Saunders, 2009; Semrud-Clikeman, 2005). More and more case studies and empirical studies are being conducted (National Research Center on Learning Disabilities, 2010), and there is great hope that this model can transform educational systems across all contents and grade levels. And indeed, when RtI is broken into its component parts and essential principles, each isolated element is validated by research (National High School Center, National Center on Response to Intervention, and Center on Instruction as part of the High School Tiered Interventions Initiative (HSTII, 2010; Mellard & Johnson, 2008; and many more).

Furthermore, the essential components and assumptions of RtI mirror the findings of *Nine Characteristics of High-Performing Schools* (Shannon, 2007). These nine items underlie many themes throughout this book:

1. A clear and shared focus
2. High standards and expectations for all students
3. Effective school leadership
4. High levels of collaboration and communication
5. Curriculum, instruction, and assessment aligned with state standards
6. Frequent monitoring of learning and teaching
7. Focused professional development
8. Supportive learning environment
9. High levels of family and community involvement

RtI is not new and it is not just for special education.

RtI has been promoted through the Office of Special Education Programs (OSEP) Center on Positive Behavior Intervention Support (PBIS), which has promoted the 80/15/5 tiered pyramid model since the 1990s as a means of organizing supports (see Figure 2.1). Clinical psychologists have utilized the central elements of progress monitoring at increasing degrees along tiers since the late 1970s. Indeed, many of the main concepts within RtI have been

FIGURE 2.1 Colorado Multi-Tiered Model of Instruction and Intervention
Source: Colorado Department of Education. www.cde.state.co.us/RtI/images/RtITriangle.png.

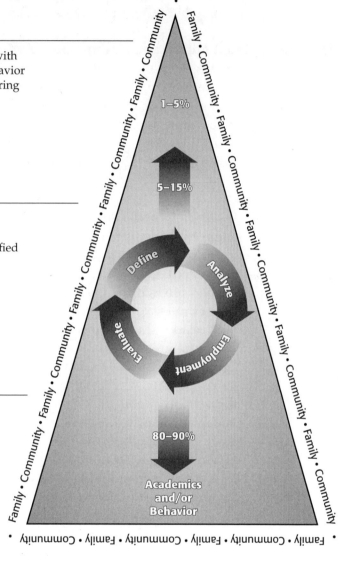

(Tier 3) Intensive Level ——————
Interventions are provided to students with intensive/chronic academic and/or behavior needs based on ongoing process monitoring and/or diagnostic assessment.

(Tier 2) Targeted Level ——————
Interventions are provided to students identified as at-risk of academic and/or social challenges and/or students identified as underachieving who require specific supports to make sufficient process in general education.

(Tier 1) Universal Level ——————
ALL students receive research-based, high quality, general education that incorporates ongoing universal screening, progress monitoring, and prescriptive assessment to design instruction. Expectations are taught, reinforced, and monitored in all settings by all adults. Discipline and other data inform the design of interventions that are preventative and proactive.

around for decades and empirically validated through applied behavior analysis and curriculum-based measures. Though the core components of RtI are not new concepts, they are not necessarily widely dispersed or fully embedded across the entire school domain. Indeed, for many schools, RtI remains primarily a special education topic. Only recently, as states grapple with how to improve overall learning outcomes, has RtI come to the forefront as a promising option for improving general education as well (Hall, 2008). An argument for RtI is at last emerging that gives the appearance that RtI really is about more than just special education. Indeed, the sooner educators think of RtI as "Response to Instruction" as well as "Response to Intervention," the smoother the entire process will be.

RtI is about both academics and behavior.

Academic issues often mingle with behavior concerns, especially in high schools. When thinking of RtI, educators must consider both "sides" of the tiered pyramid of support. Though this book does not target the behavioral side of the pyramid with as much attention as the academic side, the process and principles apply for both. A brief snapshot of our positive behavior intervention support (PBIS) follows (in order of intensity from Tier 1 through Tier 3):

♦ A well-promoted matrix of behavior expectations is reviewed and taught by students to other students.

♦ Clear expectations are taught, modeled, and recognized (celebrated) schoolwide.

♦ Teachers are informed of potential trouble spots from day one (as part of professional development) so they can increase their efforts to build relationships specifically with students who are likely to be at risk for failure.

♦ Mentorships: A robust, community-linked mentorship program has the potential to prevent at-risk students from dropping out of high school.

♦ Student-led Link Crew (see boomerangproject in reference section) to partner student leaders in the building with freshmen to ease the transition to high school.

♦ Educators use community resources and partnerships to work with students in need of support.

♦ An active dean of students tracks attendance with capacity for follow-up in order to keep attendance problems from escalating.

♦ Welcome Wagon: Laying out a warm welcome for incoming freshmen (a barbecue, orientation, partnering with junior or senior class leaders from Link Crew) and any students who join during the middle of the school year is another low-cost preventive intervention that can reduce problem behaviors and dropouts.

♦ Weekly or daily check-ins with students (from counselors, social workers, administrators, or other adult mentors in the building) reassure students that they can trust adults and that they are cared for. Also, these check-ins remind students that they are accountable for their decisions. This can be especially helpful for students with emotional concerns.

◆ A variety of social and mental health support is provided for students with the most intense needs.

RtI's assessment and intervention framework is based upon the medical model of support (triage).

At a fundamental level, RtI is a medical model applied to the educational setting. Knowing this should ease some teacher concerns that all students will be unnecessarily progress monitored in all skill areas. The intervention and assessment practice depends proportionately upon the tier of support needed for each student. The more intense the need of the student, the more intense the intervention and the more frequent the assessment of progress. Just as in the medical community, patients are tested to see if a given medical procedure has been effective: did the patient respond? Healthy patients see the doctor only occasionally for wellness checkups. Patients who are ill need more medical support more frequently and thus receive more tests. A doctor uses tests and treatments to get at the underlying cause of a health problem, and RtI asks the same of educators. Test all students initially and then twice more per year (universal screening and progress toward benchmark) to make sure they are making gains relative to peers, and then monitor grades and classroom assessments to make sure they remain "healthy" (Batsche et al., 2006). For students already behind or not progressing adequately, intervene and evaluate their progress more frequently on high school–appropriate tools (twice per month). If students are showing more significant problems, intervene even more intensely and monitor their progress weekly (and more diagnostically if necessary). The model focuses on the response to the treatment (intervention) rather than the diagnosis (special education label). This represents a vast shift in education, and schools will need time, training, and resources to make the change. A graphical demonstration of this assessment framework is in Chapter 5 (Figure 5.1 on page 41) as part of the specifics of data use across tiers.

RtI's purpose will be different between elementary and high schools and will not be the same for all states.

Given that basic background, what is the ultimate purpose of RtI for high schools? Figure 2.2 shows several authors' opinions about the purpose for RtI, specifically for high school:

RtI's purpose may not be immediately clear and defined if it is a new initiative in your state, school, or district. And the purposes set forth by others may or may not make sense in the early stages of implementation. Mellard & Johnson (2008) describe the purpose as centered on identifying and helping struggling students (as noted in Figure 2.2). According to Johnson, Smith, & Harris (2009), RtI's essential purpose is its capacity to transform systems in

FIGURE 2.2 Purpose of RtI

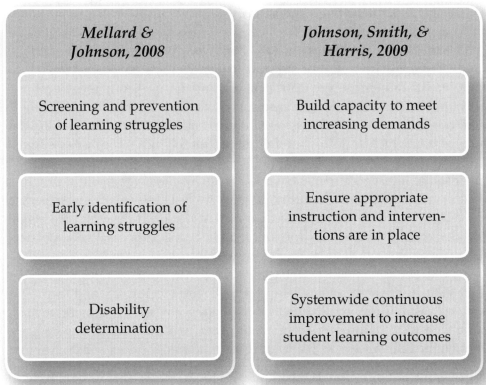

the school across all tiers. For high schools, the purpose of RtI will be a mix of both (depending on how each state deals with RtI's relationship to special education).

You know your school is "doing" RtI when . . .

RtI is not a rigid program with a clear set of guidelines for all schools to follow. In fact, many authors and researchers disagree on some of the details of RtI, such as length, duration, or intensity of intervention (Gresham, 2001; Kovaleski, 2003; Barnett, Daly, Jones & Lentz, 2004). Overall, however, there is an agreed-upon set of elements that defines what RtI looks like across settings. Researchers advocate for (and model sites employ) the following elements:

1. **High-quality, scientifically based instruction** delivered at Tier 1 meets the needs of most students (often assumed to mean 80 percent).
2. **Early, preventive interventions** are tiered to best deliver support at increasing levels of intensity based on student needs (usually three or four tiers).

3. **Data-based decision-making** drives system thinking and resource allocation, improves classroom instruction, and ensures that students are receiving proper intervention.
4. **Ongoing assessment** uses a range of instruments to measure student achievement and progress and is specifically purposed for each tier of support:
   a. **Universal screening** guides placement and predicts struggles (thus ensuring early intervention).
   b. Collection of **benchmark data** monitors student growth in curriculum and determines overall health of Tier 1 curriculum and instruction.
   c. **Progress monitoring** measures student response to intervention and measures overall effectiveness of instruction and intervention; it is administered at increasing levels of frequency corresponding to the degree of intervention intensity.
5. A **problem-solving model** is used to select, monitor, and make decisions about a student's response to intervention and to act as a gatekeeper and communicator between and within tiers of intervention.
   a. A **standard treatment protocol** (STP) should be included as an appropriate means to efficiently deliver interventions to a large group of struggling students.
   b. A **flexible support system** should also be employed to reach a targeted group of struggling students in a dynamic way.
   c. The **multidisciplinary PST** engages a wide variety of stakeholders to construct the best possible instructional plan for a student, including (but not limited to) parents and students; regular and special educators as well as interventionists; school psychologist and social worker; administrator, dean, and counselor; and possibly wraparound community support and mentors
6. **General education teachers** must take the lead for RtI to be successful (see Resources section for research support).

All these elements are necessary for RtI success, though each may look markedly different across settings. How schools choose to bring these elements to scale within the constructs of their own building culture is where RtI takes on its diverse character. Implementation of each element will depend heavily upon resources available and existing customs within buildings.

RtI implementation and maintenance require a cultural change for many high schools.

Several textbooks, websites, case studies, and articles can guide schools in implementing RtI (see Resources section; also Shores & Chester, 2009;

Mellard & Johnson, 2008; Wright, 2007; Brown-Chidsey & Steege, 2005). Some apply to all schools, and recently some have focused on high schools (including this book; also, Johnson et al., 2009; HSTII, 2010). Some target teachers specifically (Bender & Shores, 2007) and others tailor the RtI message for principals (Hall, 2008). Undoubtedly, more books about the specifics of RtI and additional research studies will be published over the coming years. Overall, however, most of the books agree that the elements listed below are key to implementation:

1. **Leadership is critical** in "creating staff consensus, delivering professional development, implementing evaluation procedures, allocating resources, making data based decisions, and creating sustainable processes" (HSTII, 2010).
   a. Leadership is shared but focused and ongoing. Strong principal-led initiative will bring a common vision into reality.
   b. Decision-makers are educated about RtI and resources are organized.
   c. A steering team creates and shares a plan to launch RtI.
   d. Leadership conducts a needs assessment (or resource inventory) to assist with resource allocation and guide professional development.
   e. A scaling-up plan will increase the degree of implementation.
   f. Principals must make RtI a general education initiative.
   g. Principals should use information feedback to improve lesson plans, the observation process, and other administrative contact with teachers.
   h. Clear expectations, monitoring of implementation, and follow-through are essential.
2. **RtI is *the* unifying initiative within the school.**
   a. Focus needs to be clearly defined and cohesive.
   b. Instructional program cohesion demands clarity (Newman, Smith, Allensworth, & Bryk, 2001).
   c. Integration of all systems in the building is essential.
3. **The culture of the building is considered as change is put into place.**
   a. Educators must be willing to change and to collaborate.
   b. The success of all students is the charge of the entire staff.
   c. Administrators must examine the changing roles of general and special education teachers.
   d. Administrators should consider implementation in stages, rather than doing everything all at once.

4. **Professional development is goal-oriented, highly focused, ongoing, and continuous.**
   a. Professional development is dedicated to the RtI framework itself and includes training in research-based instructional practices.
   b. Pre-service and in-service professional development is frequent, durable, intense enough to build skills, and offers chances for practice and discussions.
   c. Master teachers are used to support others.
5. **Professional learning communities (PLCs) will best lay the foundation for effective RtI in high schools.**
   a. Systems should be integrated, with active PLCs implementing best practices at Tier 1.
   b. Schools must ensure structural supports for professional collaboration.
   c. Assessment and instruction are aligned to standards.
6. **Community stakeholders are informed and involved in RtI implementation.**
   a. Schools should tap into network of wraparound support services and community/parent partnerships to aid with interventions.
   b. Students can take an active role in intervention selection and progress monitoring.
   c. Schools should expand communications with parents.
   d. Schools should promote high levels of family and community involvement.
7. **Limitations specific to high school implementation are considered and actively addressed.**
   a. Schools should find a way to reward credit for intervention-based classes.
   b. Changing master schedules and creative blocking may be necessary.
   c. Schools should create or locate resources to deal with the lack of research on core instructional practice for high school content and age-appropriate screening and progress-monitoring tools.
   d. Educators should find ways to creatively offer flexible interventions during the school day.
   e. Schools should create a system for fidelity assurances, providing evidence that curriculum, instruction and interventions are all high quality, research-based, and implemented consistently or RtI will not function effectively.

Make the pathway to RtI implementation efficient and meaningful.

What this book offers is a specific, consolidated, and tested pathway for high schools to practically implement the research recommendations and thoroughly embed RtI into the school's fabric. There may exist a wide variety of ways to implement RtI. One specific approach, designed to meet unique challenges in high schools, integrates the following elements:

◆ A plan for the leadership team

◆ A systematic use of to data-based decision-making across systems and tiers, with specific examples and case studies

◆ Infrastructure to implement and evaluate a tiered model of instruction and intervention that honors high school limitations

◆ The strategic and flexible use of a student support center, combined with a robust PLC culture, as the means to most efficiently and effectively deliver tiered interventions to all students

3

Challenges and Limitations for RtI in High Schools

Though most of the principles of RtI have been around for decades, synthesizing them into a cohesive approach for educational reform is a relatively recent advancement. Several schools are now shifting beyond the principles and philosophy of RtI toward the application, and the learning curve is steep. Since early implementers have been responsible for helping to grow this model to meet the needs of high school students, there are many places for innovative reforms and challenges.

RtI, at its root, is instructional reform and it is a grueling process. It may take four to eight years, and schools may reach a point where the obstacles seem insurmountable. One piece of advice: *push on*. There is hope. As noted in Chapters 1 and 2, the benefits will far outweigh the challenges. Ultimately RtI will elevate your school to a level where measurable learning outcomes are the focus of the entire building and where data-based decision-making (DBDM) informs and guides the process of continuous improvement.

RtI will increase accountability and transparency within high schools.

Herein lies the greatest challenge of RtI at the high school level: it forces schools to "look under the hood" at general classroom instruction. Through the use of data-based decision-making and an intense focus on what is working for students, the entire practice of instruction is forced to become more transparent. Increasing the transparency of instructional practices may result in resistance by teachers because it threatens their autonomy and can be personalized. Teachers' discomfort with this process notwithstanding, it is probable that some *schools* will not always like what they see when they take a discerning (data-based) look at core instruction in order to confirm its validity. For other schools, this will be a welcome challenge in which professionals work collaboratively to improve outcomes for all students.

Schools will have a variety of reactions to this challenge of RtI. Many will "close the hood" and make RtI a special education issue or argue that it does not belong in high schools. Some will try to wait it out on the sidelines, hoping either that the trend will pass or that they can avoid the mistakes of early implementers. But other high schools will valiantly tackle the significant issue of building Tier 1 capacity through data-driven instructional decision-making.

Not everyone agrees that RtI is ready for the challenge.

When viewed through the lens of preventive and tiered intervention, RtI is indeed an efficient and powerful way to guide schools toward improvement. However, if viewed as a special education initiative, the research community is not in complete agreement as to RtI's effectiveness for determining if a student has a learning disability. Many schools and districts, like ours, may have no real say in whether RtI is the only or primary way of determining a specific learning disability (SLD). It is showing up more and more in mandates at the state level, and schools are being required to join the reform movement because RtI is being presented as a special education mandate. This change, forced by the sword of special education law, is unwise and ultimately harmful to the acceptance of RtI in schools. There is no true consensus among the scholars, psychologists, and researchers in the field about RtI's ability to determine a disability. In fact, the debate taking place in education journals is ongoing. So while the experts attempt to assess the validity and reliability of this model for determining a learning disability, schools are left to implement a complex model with fidelity. In fact, based on our early experiences, this particular application of RtI certainly has its limits.

In many ways, this debate exists because the very definition of SLD is under review as many educators seek to change it. Some want to defend the integrity of the existing definition and assessment process, while others want the determining factor to be a student's responsiveness to interventions. Though this is a fairly significant point of contention, some researchers claim the debate is isolated and time-limited and believe we should take a wider perspective because the debate will be supplanted by the eventual empirical validation of RtI's vast potential (Kovaleski, 2007). Even more encouraging, a survey of the research literature also points the way to conceptual and practical consensus. Valuable elements from both camps can be agreed upon and implemented without causing panic and upheaval in high schools.

**There is room for consensus and harmony
between RtI's supporters and skeptics.**

1. The old model of SLD determination must be changed.
   a. The discrepancy model has been inappropriately used as a sole means for SLD diagnosis and must stop.
   b. A new, comprehensive model will probably include RTI *and* some IQ discrepancy measure as well as other pieces of data as a body of evidence.
   c. Evidence of deficiency against grade level benchmarks is necessary.
   d. This new way of determining SLD will demand more research for the entire framework of RtI.
2. Intense, ongoing training is needed for all staff (starting in teacher and administrator education programs, general and special education in-service training, and training for interventionists and counselors).
   a. Change is hard for buildings, but critically important.
   b. Connecting research to practice and implementation requires powerful and ongoing professional development.
3. Ensuring a quality instructional environment at all tiers is the greatest challenge but of the utmost importance because prevention and early identification of learning struggles are essential for RtI to function and because fidelity is the key to the entire process.
4. Hybrid models of problem-solving and standard treatment protocol will be the norm for high schools.

**States should be very cautious about using RtI as
the primary or only means of determining a learning
disability, especially for high school students**

Colorado has produced many valuable RtI tools and resources for other states, especially in the area of implementation and how to use RtI for determination of an SLD (LD in some states). Several of these resources are included in the Resources section of this book and as Appendix B. With that being said, other states considering or embarking upon a wholesale commitment to the RtI assessment process for SLD determination would be wise to consider carefully how the process should be used to evaluate special education eligibility at the secondary level. The nicely packaged software programs that produce goal lines and gap analysis (AIMSweb, for instance) work quite well at the elementary level, where skills are often the primary focus, but they are far from perfect for high schools. Also, elementary schools are structured in a way to allow more time for flexible grouping and intensive progress monitoring. High schools, on the other hand, dive more deeply into content and standards, and state graduation requirements are very demanding regarding content expectations.

Determining SLD through an RtI process will require new high school–level tools (that must be age-appropriate and relevant to teachers), and these are not well developed at the national level yet (though they are evolving). Protocols and a consistent model are important when it comes to special education qualification, and the norms for nondisabled students of high school age are unsound. Given some of the research-based arguments against using RtI in this manner, and based on our own early experiences, a one-size-fits-all approach to SLD eligibility across K–12 grade levels should be cautiously and meticulously examined before transitioning into an RtI-based eligibility model.

This intense, individualized model of support, assessment, and data analysis presents many practical challenges for high school educators. In theory it sounds wonderful and should be beneficial for students. Yet the intensity and specialization required to implement and document the process are a serious obstacle for most high school teachers, considering that they are working with many more students than their elementary counterparts. Couple the obstacle of the sheer volume of Tier 1 students with the actuality that many regular educators in high schools lack intervention expertise, and the challenges mount for RtI implementation as it relates to SLD diagnosis. Also, general educators usually have not been trained to interpret data or to respond in a meaningful way to help struggling students. In other words, schools have a considerable task before them in getting RtI in place, with fidelity, before it could be used to determine a disability with any degree of confidence.

High school teachers traditionally have been expertly prepared to primarily *deliver content*; the support piece has been left to special educators who have been trained to *support learning*. To get *all* teachers deeply engaged with data in a manner that can have significant impact upon instruction represents the major obstacle for RtI in high schools. This type of deliberate, meaningful change demands a fundamental shift in school culture driven by focused leadership (Johnson et al., 2009).

If RtI becomes the means of diagnosing learning disabilities in your state, high school special educators and problem-solving teams will need to be thoroughly trained in eligibility law and adaptable to the changing statutes and roles. Often in training, the proponents of RtI will claim that Tier 3 does not necessarily mean special education. Some will say that all three tiers could exist in the same classroom and that students from a variety of backgrounds could be receiving Tier 3 support. This may be true on a technical level, but practical realities in high schools will likely prove that Tier 3 mostly implies special education services (a view supported by the National Research Center on Learning Disabilities). Given the limited resources and difficulties with intensive interventions within a general education classroom, students in need of the most support will be receiving special education support. How this is structured and delivered (co-teaching, inclusion, fundamentals classes, modified or sheltered classes) will vary greatly in schools based on resources and the continuously changing federal and state special education legislation.

RtI does not have to symbolize a forced marriage of regular and special education. A possible pathway forward for the partnership between special and general educators would probably include the following elements:

- ◆ Co-teaching to build Tier 3 infrastructure (special educators modeling interventions with general educators in real time)
- ◆ Collaboration through a consult model approach in which special educators are offered expertise on differentiation of content (through professional development and professional learning communities)
- ◆ Continuing to offer a continuum of courses to reach a wide variety of student needs
- ◆ Regular collaboration with problem-solving teams, the school psychologist, and RtI teams to inform best practices, differentiation, and intervention options.

High schools that implement RtI face unique challenges.

Some of the challenges unique to high schools are based on the significant differences between the elementary and secondary settings (Sugai, 2004):

- ◆ **Changes in organizational structure**: High school offers more content specializations and less individual attention, so at-risk students go undetected more easily. Staff meeting times are less available; there is less fidelity of professional development.
- ◆ **Shift in academic focus:** High schools move beyond skills into application, beyond supportive learning and direct instruction into independent learning across multiple contents, with an expectation of self-monitoring and motivation.
- ◆ **Nonschool responsibilities**: Teenagers are working, dating, driving, and are more distracted than elementary school students.

Further challenges exist across the high school setting, as noted by the HSTII (2010) team:

◆ **Staff capacity:** Schools must build in time to collaborate and continually learn RtI and data-based decision-making.

◆ **Scheduling:** Successful schools acknowledge the inherent complexities of high school scheduling regarding tiered interventions and are willing to adjust the master schedule. Delivering intervention support often means that students will lose elective options.

◆ **Resources:** All schools noted that creativity was the key, but resource allocation for RtI was difficult.

◆ **Fidelity:** All schools agreed that monitoring instruction and intervention was a significant challenge.

Based on our own experience, high schools face additional challenges, especially in states where RtI is the primary means by which a learning disability is diagnosed:

◆ Collecting benchmark data from high school students will increase the already high degree of test fatigue (state tests, national tests, content level tests, college readiness tests, etc.).

◆ The students most in need of remediation will have fewer elective classes, will be more resistant to support, and are often those with attendance, engagement, and apathy problems. These variables dramatically complicate addressing the root academic concern.

◆ Not all schools have the means to provide small-group instruction to those students below benchmarks, especially if the assistance is not linked to classroom grades (a lack of buy-in for students); schools also may lack time to fit skill-based remediation into the school day for those trying to gather credits on their way toward graduation.

◆ High schools will probably need to redefine the roles of general and special educators and involve the expertise of special educators much earlier in the intense intervention and data collection process.

◆ Schools will need to be extra-vigilant in not allowing RtI to delay special education services for those in need. In our system, we do not wait to label a student with a disability prior to providing services because the process is often slow and students must not be denied services due to RtI's lengthy evaluation process (early court cases have ruled in favor of schools in this manner, however; see Burns, Jacob, & Wagner, 2007, commentary on *Johnson v. Upland*, 2002).

◆ High schools have an urgent and varied constellation of concerns and to address only one element at a time may not be enough. Depending on each state's particular level of urgency, districts and schools might need to build and fine-tune the entire plane while flying it, a frightening prospect indeed. Though researchers (Johnson et al., 2009) recommend implementing RtI in stages over time, for many districts the needs are too urgent to address in a piecemeal way.

The longer high schools wait to implement RtI, the more difficult it will be.

A piece of advice for those holding back: be an early implementer. You will be much further ahead (and thankful for it) as you will have a bigger voice in the destiny of RtI in your district.

- ◆ Educate a core team. Attend conferences and schedule site visits to mature implementer sites in order to gain further knowledge and collaborate with experienced RtI educators.
- ◆ Contribute ideas and shape the process. Become involved with form development, help establish protocols, and review data management systems that your district is considering. This will allow you to have input and thus the forms will be more user-friendly at your site.
- ◆ Collaborate outside of your setting. Partner with other local high schools through high school RtI "summits" in which you share struggles, best practices for RtI, and next steps.
- ◆ Be prepared to share your process (not just the end product) with all stakeholders.

Conclusion

The first three chapters have highlighted the hopes and challenges of RtI derived from both research and our own experience as an early high school implementer. The remainder of this book is dedicated to presenting a streamlined approach for bringing RtI to scale in your high school.

4

A Recommended Pathway for Implementing and Maintaining RtI at the High School Level

RtI, though complicated and arduous, is certain to be a rewarding and effective undertaking. Schools do not, however, have to start creating RtI from scratch. At least some of the components are in place, even if in infancy, loosely connected, or unaligned. For instance, educators already use lots of data, participate in professional development, care about students, intervene to help struggling kids, and work collaboratively to achieve goals. But are the data used effectively and meaningfully to improve learning outcomes? Are the goals and systems aligned and focused? Ultimately, the challenge for schools implementing RtI is aligning all the programs, goals, collaboration, planning, and data dialogues into a cohesive approach to continuous, systemic school improvement. Furthermore, the researchers referenced in the previous chapters accurately point to fidelity (of curriculum, instruction and intervention as verified by administrators) as being both the linchpin and the most challenging part of RtI to get right. After years of struggle, our school has arrived at a way to improve the constructs of fidelity within our RtI process. This chapter will outline this expectation, and the following four chapters will explore the construct of fidelity in greater detail.

Recommended Pathway for RTI Implementation

The following pathway is not meant to be overly prescriptive nor so generic as to be irrelevant. Since education is a local affair, many of the details will need to be worked out by individual departments, buildings, districts, and states. No matter what some books claim, this will not be easy. Even with the following recommendations, this process will not be concise and simple. Consider the following as guiding elements that are worth emphasizing as you roll up your sleeves.

There are many ways for high schools to package and bring to scale all the elements and implementation steps listed in Chapter 2. Each school will need to digest all the available advice and forge a plan that honors its own unique setting while also including the critical aspects. Expediting implementation will demand that leadership initially handpick and empower an RtI leadership team.

The RtI Leadership Team

High school principals and assistant principals are often responsible for hiring, evaluation, discipline, attendance, bureaucracy, budgeting, crisis management, and staff development. There are many priorities competing for their attention, and RtI poses an additional and significant undertaking. Principals will need time to fully comprehend and assign resources to prepare the school for the challenges that lie in store. Specifically, RtI requires principals to be instructional leaders in the building to ensure fidelity of instruction. To facilitate this responsibility, they will need to commit to data-based decision-making that leads to improved outcomes. Principals must also be effective delegators and collaborators as they build consensus and ownership for systemic change in their buildings.

The RtI leadership team should be handpicked and consist of a diverse cluster of building leaders (depending on each building's structures):

- ◆ Principal and other administration officials (vice or assistant principals, deans)
- ◆ Counselors
- ◆ Department chairs and possibly professional learning community leaders from all content areas
- ◆ Data processing expert, assessment specialist, and/or technical support
- ◆ Math and literacy interventionists

◆ Special education leadership (and school psychologist when possible)

The RtI leadership team will have to perform two parallel missions: implementing RtI buildingwide and undertaking system evaluation that aligns professional development. It took our school about five years to make this shift, but I would argue that the shift should occur sooner.

Three Big Ideas and Essential Tasks for the RtI Leadership Team

1. Study and plan collaboratively how RtI will develop in your school; monitor, adjust, and share the implementation.
2. Embed data-based decision-making across all systems to build the construct of fidelity, ensuring a strong foundation for RtI. Conduct a regular needs assessment of all systems and use a rubric and resource inventory that guides professional development.
3. Establish a tiered model of instruction and intervention.
   a. Use a hybrid model of problem-solving and standard treatment protocol.
   b. Allocate resources for a student support center to become the hub of flexible intervention delivery.
   c. Use professional learning communities and standards-based methods of assessment and grading.

A visual demonstration of these priorities follows in Figure 4.1.

The three Big Ideas must align and converge upon student learning, as demonstrated by data, for effective implementation. Systems must work together; RtI is the cohesive mechanism that moves schools beyond piecemeal change (Johnson et al. 2009). Deep change demands that schools move beyond the complacent routine of "random acts of improvement" toward a cohesive improvement pathway.

The three Big Ideas are prioritized and roughly chronological, but they are not mutually exclusive because RtI is not an isolated process. If schools have the luxury of time to initiate a five-year process (which is ideal), these elements can be systematically phased in. However, even though different schools are starting at different points, all elements must be implemented at some point, regardless of how they are phased in. There are implicit dangers in proceeding too slowly and in proceeding too fast. Moving forward at the appropriate pace in a strategic manner (as established by the RtI leadership team) will set the stage for success.

FIGURE 4.1 Leadership Responsibilities

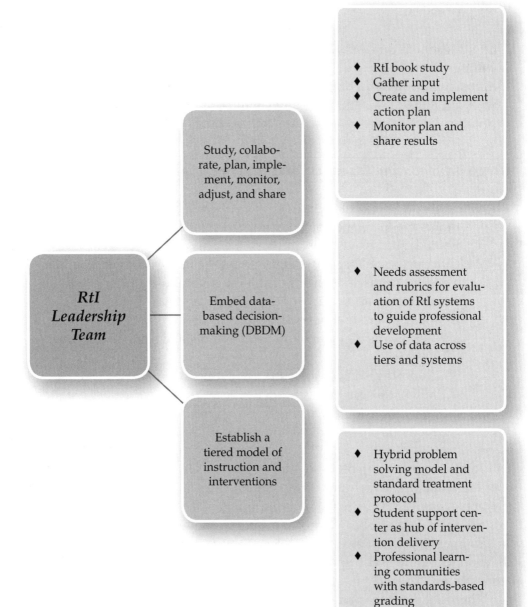

Big Idea 1: Collaboration

Exploration and Adoption of RtI

There are many ways to explore and access recommendations about the RtI process thanks to the burgeoning market of resources. This book is not alone, but one of a variety of resources leadership teams should reference. This book (or others) can be used for a book study in which the leadership team would examine how its recommendations could fit into current structures. Most importantly, the leadership team should look for elements that are already in place and that could be enhanced without reinventing the wheel. Many of the figures displayed throughout this book are available through the publisher's website. Before, during, and after a book study, the team members should also attend as many conferences, trainings, and site visits to other high schools as possible, with time to digest, process, and plan steps for your school.

Right from the start, the team should perform as a professional learning community with established norms, a shared vision, and an immersion in data-based decision-making. As your team attends various training opportunities, consider the following guiding questions that are likely to expose key areas for improvement and drive an improvement plan:

1. How will you know if your instruction, curriculum, and assessments are of the highest quality? What will you do if they are not?
2. Assuming the instruction, curriculum, grading, and assessments are of the highest quality, how will you intervene if students still are not progressing?
3. How will you measure and track the effectiveness of the intervention?
4. Who will be in charge of oversight of school improvement (making sure all systems are effective and aligned)?
5. What degree of resistance to RtI can be anticipated and possibly assuaged?

The construction of an implementation plan need not be complex, but it should involve a distributed model of leadership, involving active department chairs and empowered teacher-leaders. Though the model itself should not be considered optional, how it is constructed and implemented should include input from the entire staff.

After the leadership team has conducted an extensive book study and anticipated points of contention and implementation challenges unique to the school, a larger book study, led by the leadership team, should be conducted for the entire staff. This expanded book study should include many breakout sessions (facilitating small-group discussions) and constitute the faculty's professional development for an entire semester (or year). Offering an RtI book study communicates that the leadership team has made RtI a leading priority, especially if the staff is aware that the book study will also foster input from everyone in driving the schoolwide improvement plan.

Study groups should consider the three Big Ideas as themes in need of more specificity within each department, all the while looking for elements already in place. Too often, teachers are not given the opportunity to understand schoolwide initiatives prior to implementation. Open discussion and input must be valued in the process. Immersing an entire staff in the topic of RtI and encouraging discussion will increase ownership of implementation across all settings.

Improvement Plan

This book assumes that high schools are versed in the topic of improvement plans (or action plans) as part of the planning and improvement process. Furthermore, that the goals of a team are SMART (Specific, Measurable, Attainable, Relevant, and Time-bound), as suggested by Conzemius & O'Neill (2001, Chapter 2), is a bare minimal requirement and likely already understood by educational leaders. The development of action plans helps to organize thinking, prioritize needs, allocate resources, assign responsibility, establish timelines, and monitor goal attainment. The forms used to guide improvement can range in complexity and efficiency, but the last component, monitoring, is most challenging. It is generally most difficult to actually evaluate the action plan to make sure the agreed-upon goals are being met. Often educators and administrators spend the bulk of their time looking ahead because such forward thinking becomes critical to survival. But without time to review action plans, the message will be clear: the school does not really value the process of data-based decision-making. This must become a leading priority if continuous improvement is to be embedded in a school's culture.

One of the central tasks of school leaders is the delivery of information feedback to staff (Noell & Gansle, 2006), including how schools are progressing toward goals. Therefore it is essential that the improvement plan and subsequent results should be shared with all stakeholders, including the community, parents, students, and staff, on a frequent basis (perhaps every semester or quarter, depending on established timeliness). By sharing and posting this reflective and iterative process of data-based decision-making, the RtI leadership team demonstrates the process and the importance of monitoring and adjusting even the implementation of RtI. Furthermore, the leadership team provides the model by which all systems are to work with improvement plans and data, from PLCs to problem-solving teams and special education, and this becomes the unifying vision for improving outcomes.

The very iterative and data-based nature of this sharing and reviewing will foster the transition from implementation into evaluation, maintenance, and improvement. Also, the more we share our process and results, the more we demand from ourselves and insist upon improvement across all systems. As you read the following chapters, consider the natural shift from implementation into improvement.

Sharing the RtI Process Across All Tiers with All Stakeholders

At each step of development, schools should dedicate some portion of their creative energy to promoting and sharing the RtI process. Sharing the process will minimize confusion about RtI in your school and will incorporate parents as allies in the subsequent growth and development. Here are some possible ways to communicate with community and staff about the RtI process:

- ◆ pamphlets
- ◆ parent nights (open houses)
- ◆ website
- ◆ libraries of resources
- ◆ staff training
- ◆ advisory accountability meetings with parents

For our school, the centerpiece of promoting RtI (both academically and behaviorally) is a web link on our school web page showcasing our RtI process, including forms, intervention rubrics, and a glossary of terms and acronyms (see Resources section). Also, we include links to national and state policies and to other informative websites about RtI in general. As a team, we present information about how RtI functions in our high school to the community during parent nights and open houses. Furthermore, we report annually to our school advisory and accountability team, composed of community members, presenting evidence of our success. This is an ideal forum for sharing data and the implicit complexities and challenges of implementing RtI at the high school level.

Conclusion

The RtI leadership team has significant tasks that are very demanding. As it works to build, collaborate, and share a plan, it is also working to ensure fidelity and a tiered framework for interventions. Each item in isolation could be overwhelming. This is why the team must focus upon a common goal and share the results with all stakeholders regularly. RtI requires much of the school leadership, which in turn requires much of the staff members who must ultimately implement it.

The following chapters deepen the discussion about the next two Big Ideas, embedding data-based decision-making and establishing a tiered model of instruction and intervention.

5

Data-Based Decision-Making Embedded across Systems and Tiers

As noted in previous chapters, data-based decision-making (DBDM) is the key mechanism by which RtI functions in a school. It must guide the work of all systems and structures if the school is to establish a culture of continuous improvement. DBDM should be used to evaluate and respond across all school domains. In order to again reconceptualize RtI as "Response to *Information*,"(in addition to "Intervention" and "Instruction") school districts must streamline the process, ideally through a highly efficient data management system, with time scheduled into the school year to evaluate and respond to the data. To create this time, high schools should utilize quarterly "data days" to evaluate the effectiveness of programs and should apply consistent analysis of data during professional learning community (PLC) meetings.

Improving a school's relationship with data requires that we strive to maximize data's value. At what stage is your school in its relationship with data?

Stage 1: Which data?
Stage 2: Collecting data
Stage 3: Analyzing some parcels of data for a few consumers
Stage 4: Storing the analyzed data
Stage 5: Sharing the analyzed data with all stakeholders
Stage 6: Sharing and responding to analyzed data with all stakeholders most of the time
Stage 7: Data transparency and responsiveness is embedded in all school endeavors regarding student achievement

To reach stage 7 of the data pyramid requires the polarization of two competing cultures, in which sensitivity and anxiety are low and professionalism and trust are high. When decisions within a school are consistently and transparently based on data and when the culture is trusting, true DBDM is the result.

One leading proponent of RtI, George Batsche, who has worked to implement RtI in Florida for years, heavily emphasizes the need for a powerful data management system on top of carefully constructed assessment frameworks and the use of quarterly data days. He is also process-oriented and leads many RtI conferences across the nation. One fruit of Batsche's labors is the following assessment flow chart (Figure 5.1) (Martinez & Batsche, 2008), demonstrating how standard treatment protocol and problem-solving models can construct a body of evidence that reflects student learning. Most flow charts in RtI are frighteningly complex and bewildering. This is one of the simplest and most concise you will find as it strips the pyramid into treatment and assessment steps.

Though schools can use a wide variety of data, the RtI literature offers established guidelines on *when* to use the data. This is especially true in using RtI to determine specific learning disabilities (SLD). The National Research Center on Learning Disabilities (NRCLD) points to research suggesting that a Tier 2 intervention last for eight to twelve weeks, monitored via curriculum-based measures (CBM) about twice per month. A Tier 3 intervention consists of more intensive support over an even greater period of time, with progress monitoring weekly. Though there is no clear consensus yet in the research literature which specifies these parameters further for high schools, the decisions made between tiers by the problem-solving team will be covered in some detail in Chapter 8. Ultimately, however, creating a concrete set of expectations (cut scores or decision rules) for data reviews, durations, and frequencies will be a district- or state-level decision.

When we began to take an inventory of data collection and analysis in our building, we discovered that several of us were doing the same data analysis without sharing it with the right people (double work!). To increase efficiency, we developed a table of what data each group was collecting and using across tiers. Furthermore, we worked to establish expectations (who, what, and when) for how DBDM was to occur across all tiers. Much of this effort is summarized in Figure 5.1 and more fully developed at various places in the rest of the book. Look for the following DBDM icon to highlight specific examples of the use of data to drive decision-making:

DBDM

FIGURE 5.1 Assessment Flow Chart
Source: Martinez & Batsche, 2008.

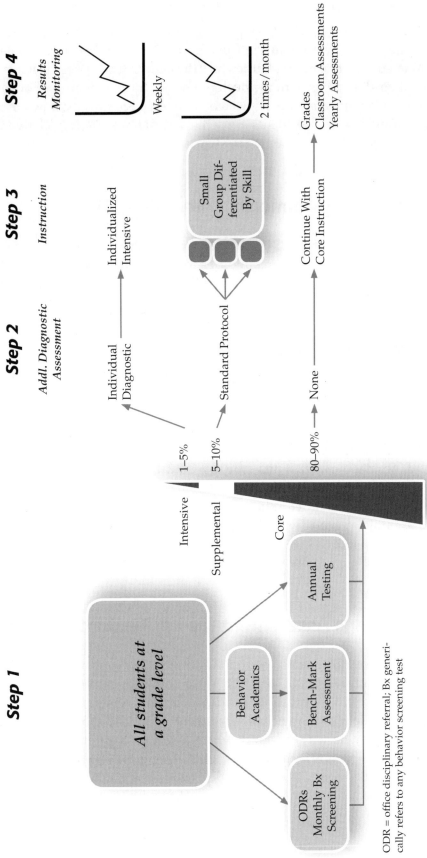

ODR = office disciplinary referral; Bx generi-
cally refers to any behavior screening test

One goal of creating the table in Figure 5.2 is to ensure that all systems are evaluated systemically and efficiently through DBDM. When schools inventory their data collection, they often discover duplication of effort in some areas while other areas are neglected altogether. Specifically, how are schools measuring how well students are achieving *and* progressing relative to their peers (nationally, locally, or at the state level)?

Systemically Embedding DBDM

Some researchers, such as Kovaleski and Glew (2006), suggest forming separate data analysis teams in order to deepen the role of data in schools. Though for the sake of efficiency the RtI leadership team and the problem-solving team in our school jointly fulfill this role, the expectations are the same. Such teams should be comprised of a diverse membership and follow Schmoker's (2002) process in which teams focus attention on benchmark data, set goals, select strategies, and monitor goal attainment.

The following flow chart (Figure 5.3 on page 47) is a demonstration of our school's model, which includes four key steps listed below and outlined throughout this chapter:

1. Undertake a needs assessment to prioritize what must be addressed.
2. Undertake a data dialogue to review last year's strengths and weaknesses (with an improvement plan) and share current year's screening data in order to intervene early.
3. Train staff on Tier 1 strategies to help at-risk students in the classroom (see discussion of professional development in Chapter 6).
4. Follow up, share ideas, and evaluate the impact of interventions.

The Needs Assessment (as RtI Resource Inventory)

Administrators should have PLCs conduct a needs assessment near the conclusion of the school year. PLCs are knowledgeable about content and assessment but will probably need additional oversight by administration to ensure fidelity of the needs assessment. Evidence should be required (in a nonthreatening way) to show where PLC teams are in the process of RtI (assessments, progress-monitoring tools, strategies used, PLC or department minutes, and grade book samples). The needs assessment should be compiled and analyzed to find common needs that require professional development

FIGURE 5.2. Data-Based Decision-Making across Tiers

	Tier 1 (Universal)	Tier 2 (Strategic)	Tier 3 (Intensive)
RtI Leadership & Administrators 1. Gauge health of all systems of instruction, curriculum, and interventions 2. Ensure school is making adequate progress and adjust accordingly 3. Set clear schoolwide goals; monitor and share results 4. Use individual classroom data to help teachers improve learning outcomes 5. Use professional development to reach goals and embed DBDM into school culture	Behavior (ODRs, SET report, attendance) Standardized test scores (state and/or national, schoolwide (historical) and compared to other schools Longitudinal growth data (see Colorado model in Figure 5.3) Benchmark data, schoolwide Workforce and postsecondary readiness Credits, GPAs, graduation rates Advanced course success rates and demographics (AP and IB exams) Demographic analysis overall Student involvement (athletics, clubs) Longitudinal growth and performance data to be reviewed with each teacher as part of evaluation process and to guide professional development Use of needs assessment (rubric) to monitor systems	Overview of all strategic intervention classes: Failure rates Percentage of students reaching benchmark with support Overall achievement gap analysis, including growth and proficiency (see Colorado model in Figure 5.3) Use of evaluation rubric to improve strategic intervention classes	Overview of all intense intervention classes: Failure rates Percentage of students reaching benchmark with support up to and including special education services Overall achievement gap analysis, including growth and proficiency (see Colorado model in Figure 5.3) Use of evaluation rubric to improve intensive intervention classes Percentage of students with disabilities reaching benchmark goals (for achievement and progress)

FIGURE 5.2. Data-Based Decision-Making across Tiers *(continued)*

	Tier 1 (*Universal*)	Tier 2 (*Strategic*)	Tier 3 (*Intensive*)
Problem-Solving Team 1. Guide placement into STP interventions 2. Share risk data with all staff 3. Gauge student responsiveness to interventions and adjust accordingly 4. Handle all referrals	Classroom failure rates Overall failure rates, buildingwide	Placement into STP based on multiple data points (standard, common, anecdotal, classroom, engagement, etc.) Success of students in intervention classes Impact of intervention upon benchmark proficiency Use of data (class common assessments and progress monitoring tools) to identify students who are not succeeding with Tier 1 and 2 support	Use of targeted progress monitoring tools to measure responsiveness to increasing intensity of intervention In partnership with special education, use of more diagnostic assessments and nationally normed progress monitoring tools to intensify intervention support Use of cut scores, goal lines, and gap analysis if determination of disability is appropriate

FIGURE 5.2. Data-Based Decision-Making across Tiers *(continued)*

	Tier 1 (Universal)	Tier 2 (Strategic)	Tier 3 (Intensive)
Professional Learning Communities and/ or Departments 1. Use common assessments to improve outcomes (learn from each other) 2. Make curricular and/or pedagogical adjustments based on data 3. Use benchmark screening data to anticipate, prevent, and guide response to struggles. 4. Use Power Standards to teach most meaningful content in depth	Use of common, formative assessment results and progress monitoring to highlight places of success and to adjust curriculum Use of classroom grade data to align grading practices (standards-based grading to minimize grade inconsistency) Vertical articulation (students progressing at grade level pace) Assessments (state, benchmark, district level)—historical Growth and performance within a department or content area	Partner with intervention classes to focus on essential understandings and access to core curriculum Use common curriculum and grading to identify students who are not meeting benchmark or not progressing Embed remediation and acceleration opportunities into general curriculum to help all students	Partner with interventionist to ensure access to and progress in common curriculum (essential understandings) Offer modifications to core curriculum as needed for students who qualify

FIGURE 5.2. Data-Based Decision-Making across Tiers *(continued)*

	Tier 1 (*Universal*)	Tier 2 (*Strategic*)	Tier 3 (*Intensive*)
General Educators 1. Be responsive to achievement data and growth data 2. Use data from formative and summative assessments to improve teaching	Differentiate in classroom based on Big Ideas (remediation and acceleration) Provide accommodations as necessary to meet needs of all students Use benchmark and common assessment data for strategic grouping	Partner with interventionist to use progress monitoring data to inform instruction (help all by helping the few) Embed remediation into instruction	Modify as necessary to meet needs of students Partner with interventionist to use progress monitoring data to inform instruction
Interventionists and Special Educators 1. Be responsive to trend lines and gap analysis	Use benchmark data and common assessments to gauge student's responsiveness to intervention support Partner with general educators to embed remediation opportunities and improve curriculum access	Use progress monitoring data to target strategic intervention Use evaluation rubric to improve intervention classes	Use evaluation rubric to improve intervention classes (and adjust as needed) In partnership with PST, use more diagnostic assessments and nationally normed progress monitoring tools to specify intervention support Use cut scores, goal lines, and gap analysis if determination of disability is appropriate

FIGURE 5.3 Embedding DBDM into Tier I

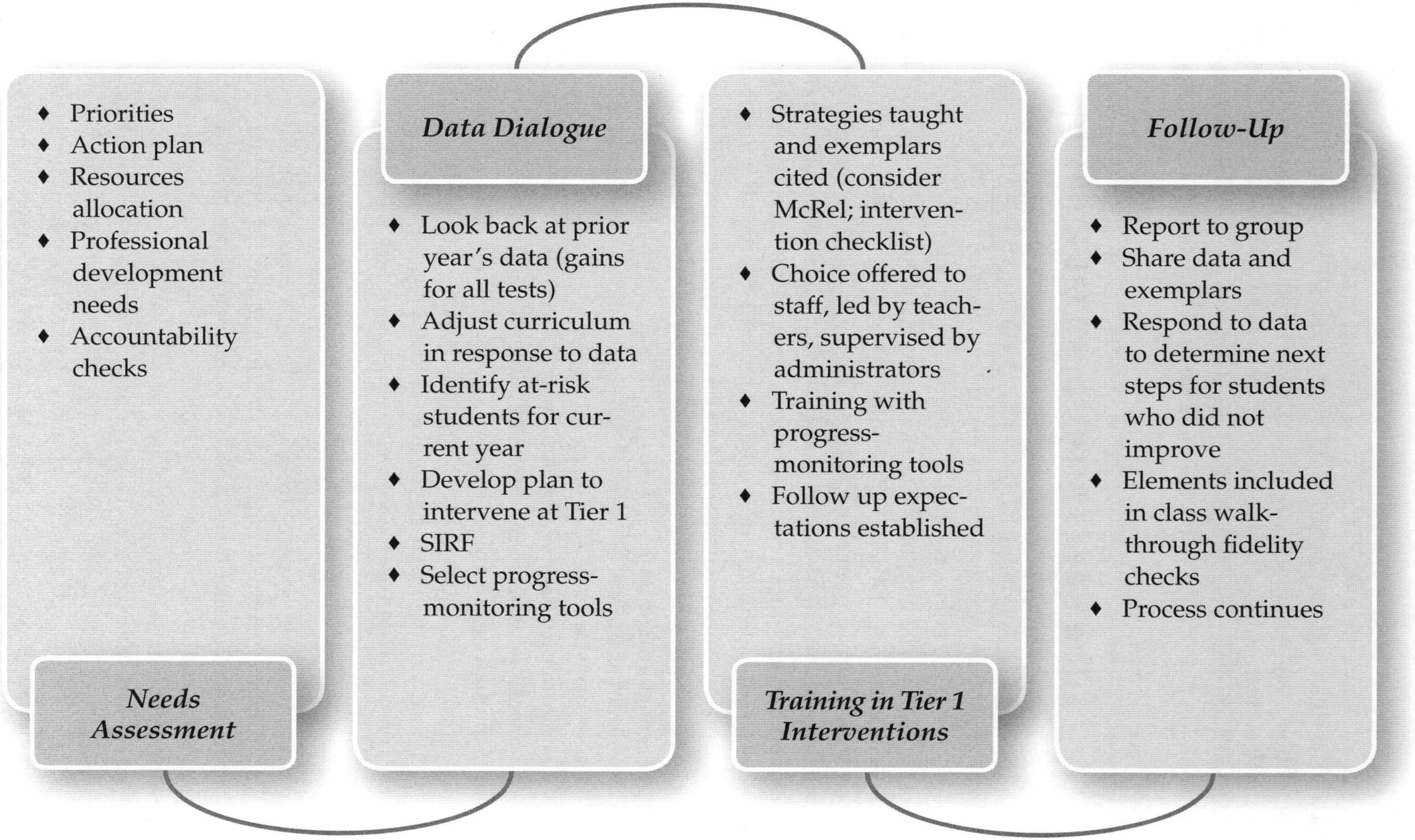

Needs Assessment

- Priorities
- Action plan
- Resources allocation
- Professional development needs
- Accountability checks

Data Dialogue

- Look back at prior year's data (gains for all tests)
- Adjust curriculum in response to data
- Identify at-risk students for current year
- Develop plan to intervene at Tier 1 SIRF
- Select progress-monitoring tools

Training in Tier 1 Interventions

- Strategies taught and exemplars cited (consider McRel; intervention checklist)
- Choice offered to staff, led by teachers, supervised by administrators
- Training with progress-monitoring tools
- Follow up expectations established

Follow-Up

- Report to group
- Share data and exemplars
- Respond to data to determine next steps for students who did not improve
- Elements included in class walk-through fidelity checks
- Process continues

across all contents and PLCs. Indeed, when teams review screening data and plan instructional practices (Kovaleski and Pedersen, 2008), it results in schools improving goal attainment. Focus of professional development is critical: educators have far too many ideas but little attention is paid to those that work (Kovaleski, 2007). All of these demands require that schools have a solid action plan in place and the means to monitor progress toward goals.

The Needs Assessment (as Rubric)

The needs assessment became transformative once we utilized it as a rubric of expectations as well as a resource inventory (see Figure 5.4). It ultimately served to guide our implementation action plan and then set the stage for professional development (see Resources section for the National Research Center on Learning Disabilities version). Though it is desirable to complete one of these forms for each department (and/or PLC), one compiled for the entire school will help inform comprehensive professional development. Thus this also becomes a document to be reviewed by the leadership team as it seeks to improve instruction, curriculum, and intervention delivery.

The purpose of a needs assessment (as rubric and resource inventory) is to:

◆ gauge readiness
◆ establish targets
◆ set priorities and allocate resources
◆ inform professional development
◆ monitor curriculum, instruction, interventions, and special education through data analysis (grades, CBMs, standardized and benchmark measures), rubrics, surveys (parent, teacher, student), and frequent observation with behavioral checklists
◆ ensure that proper documentation across tiers is in place to satisfy all mandates and accountability requirements

Within our building, we transformed the needs assessment into a more usable rubric of expectations. This document should not just be dropped into the laps of departments and PLCs. Rather it should serve as a tool to enhance the dialogue about best practices and schoolwide goals. The rubric has the potential to help all staff members grasp the vision and direction for improvement since it has built-in avenues for feedback to drive improvement of instruction, curriculum, and interventions. Our edits to this document are based on research principles and best practices, but it is not an exhaustive review of buildingwide policies. Schools will likely find it helpful to

FIGURE 5.4. Needs Assessment as a Rubric

Department Grade Level ___	Beginning (1)	Intermediate (2)	Advanced (3)	Evidence to be provided (later, with administrative team)	Resources needed in order to improve
1. Curriculum & Instructional Delivery	◆ Reluctance to explicitly teach specific reading, writing, and/or math standards ◆ Curriculum partially aligned to standards or district pacing guide ◆ Teachers not aligned within PLC (sole proprietors) ◆ Unit plans are not formalized ◆ Lesson plans are inadequate to meet curriculum expectations or guide instructional delivery ◆ No evidence of understanding-by-design (UBD) principles ◆ Big Ideas are not evident in most units ◆ Instruction is limited to one modality of learning ◆ Instruction is limited to one primary delivery such as lecture, worksheets, or textbook ◆ Little higher-level thinking is required of students ◆ Assessments planned after unit is designed and are generally based on memorization and recall, lacking rigor, relevance, and higher-level thinking	◆ Beginning to discuss how to teach specific reading, writing, and/or math standards ◆ Most elements of curriculum are aligned to standards and pacing guide ◆ Most teachers are aligned within PLC ◆ Unit plans are developed ◆ Lesson plans meet curriculum expectations ◆ Some units employ UBD principles ◆ Big Ideas are in place for most units; students are informed of Big Ideas ◆ A few teaching modalities are featured ◆ Instructional delivery usually includes multiple strategies such as group work, presentation, discussions, simulations, etc. ◆ Some higher-level thinking required of students ◆ Rigor and relevance are evident in some assignments ◆ Assessments are based on predetermined student outcomes and include multiple levels of questioning	◆ Attention is explicitly given to teaching specific reading, writing, and/or math standards no matter what the content ◆ Curriculum is clearly aligned to standards and district pacing guide ◆ Common curriculum across all PLCs; common instructional language across all PLCs ◆ Coherent and organized materials (precise unit plans) ◆ Common lesson plans guide instructional delivery ◆ UBD principles employed throughout entire curriculum ◆ Big Ideas are shared and reviewed to keep students abreast of the purpose of the unit; students understand their connection to daily instruction ◆ Multiple teaching modalities embedded ◆ Instructional delivery is engaging, relevant, scaffolded, and differentiated for student learning ◆ Uses variety of materials (text, supplemental, technology ◆ Higher-level thinking emphasized (Bloom's taxonomy) ◆ Rigor and relevance are evident across entire curriculum ◆ Assessments are a result of the backward design model, include multiple levels of questioning, and correlate to standards for student learning	Course overview and syllabus Big Ideas and/or themes Sample unit assignments, labs, homework, and materials	Initial status Quarter 1 status: _____ Quarter 2 status: _____ Quarter 3 status: _____ End of year status: _____

FIGURE 5.4. Needs Assessment as a Rubric *(continued)*

Department _____ Grade Level _____	Beginning (1)	Intermediate (2)	Advanced (3)	Evidence to be provided (later, with administrative team)	Resources needed in order to improve
2. Strategies & Interventions to Support Curriculum	◆ No strategic review of material is in place for essential content/skills ◆ Research-based strategies not in place ◆ Infrequent use of strategies and/or interventions; Tier 1 interventions lacking ◆ Little or no differentiation is offered (for G/T, ELL, or IEP) ◆ Once a concept is taught, students have no second opportunity to attain proficiency ◆ Assessments are summative with little response to the data ◆ Remediation concerns are not addressed ◆ No plan in place to provide intervention; lack of working relationship with intervention resources in the building	◆ Review of a few essential content/skill elements ◆ Some research-based strategies (McREL) in place ◆ First steps for improving Tier 1 interventions are in place ◆ Differentiation is employed for a few activities and units (for G/T, ELL, or IEP) ◆ Students can retake some tests or demonstrate mastery in other ways ◆ Some formative assessments have been developed and data are collected ◆ Needed supports to address remediation are identified ◆ Partnership with SSC (or other intervention resources) mostly involves work completion and makeup work	◆ Spiral review of essential content/skills ◆ Research-based best practices (McREL) evident in daily instruction and outlined and embedded in each unit (link to resources) ◆ Tier 1 interventions are clearly understood and applied ◆ Differentiation strategies are commonly in place throughout the unit as needed ◆ Formative opportunities (multiple chances or means) exist for students to demonstrate proficiency on the majority of standards or units ◆ Data from formative assessments are used to inform instruction and improve interventions ◆ Opportunities for remediation in place ◆ Partnership with SSC (or other intervention resources) is focused on remediating skill deficiencies, reaching proficiency, and responding to classroom data ◆ Co-teaching has been in place for more than one year (involving at least two members of the PLC) and an improvement plan is in place for next year	Essential skills and strategies employed Intervention menu PLC minutes Student Support Center (SSC) feedback	Initial status Quarter 1 status: _____ Quarter 2 status: _____ Quarter 3 status: _____ End of year status: _____

FIGURE 5.4. Needs Assessment as a Rubric *(continued)*

Department Grade Level ___	Beginning (1)	Intermediate (2)	Advanced (3)	Evidence to be provided (later, with administrative team)	Resources needed in order to improve
3. Use of Data to Inform Instruction	◆ Uses data a few times per year to decide if curriculum and instruction are working ◆ No review of previous year's data ◆ Use of incoming student data is minimal ◆ Little or no time set aside for reflection and curriculum improvements ◆ Cursory examination of test data on a quarterly basis to see how students are doing ◆ Review of class averages (mean grade percent) to see how students are doing ◆ Little or no discussion of D/F percentages across PLC or across classrooms	◆ Uses data a few times per semester to decide if curriculum and instruction are working ◆ Review and discussion of previous year's data ◆ General review of data for incoming students to gauge strengths and weaknesses ◆ Some time set aside to make improvements to existing curriculum though the use of data ◆ Review of most tests and some specific items to determine effectiveness of curriculum ◆ Quarterly review of D/F percentages with discussion	◆ Uses data at least monthly to action-ably respond, reflect, and adjust plans to increase student learning ◆ Reflects on previous year's data to evaluate effectiveness of curriculum and instruction and make adjustments as necessary ◆ A formal intervention plan (like a SIRF) is in place for responding to incoming student data ◆ Targeted use of screening data from day one to inform instruction and curriculum ◆ Consistent use of data for every unit to improve curriculum and instruction (curriculum improvement plans in place) ◆ Item analysis of test questions used to systematically improve curriculum and instruction (for every unit) ◆ Monthly review of D/F percentages including a plan to respond to high failure rates (such as remediation, increased use of formative assessment, curriculum adjustments, engagement and motivation interventions, increased focus on relevance and relationships, parent conferences, etc.)	Formative assessments; unit tests (re-teaching?) Unit improvement plans PLC minutes about data responsiveness D/F data lists	Initial status Quarter 1 status: _____ _____ Quarter 2 status: _____ _____ Quarter 3 status: _____ _____ End of year status: _____

FIGURE 5.4. Needs Assessment as a Rubric *(continued)*

Department Grade Level ___	Beginning (1)	Intermediate (2)	Advanced (3)	Evidence to be provided (later, with administrative team)	Resources needed in order to improve
4. Progress Monitoring	◆ No systemic progress monitoring through tools such CBMs is in place or in development ◆ Dialogue has not begun about what skills to monitor ◆ Students not responsible for tracking any data ◆ No infrastructure in place to support progress monitoring ◆ Assessment data does not impact instruction	◆ Discussion around CBMs is beginning; skills/standards to be monitored are identified ◆ Sample questions are written ◆ Students track some element of their progress or performance in class ◆ Administration protocol and process forming ◆ CBMs are being developed or used, but no explicit plan for remediation is in place	◆ CBMs developed to monitor progress monthly (Tier 1) and every two weeks (Tier 2) ◆ Skills to be monitored are clearly identified in lesson plans and evident in classroom instruction ◆ Students self-track and monitor progress in a data folder (for Tier 2 interventions) ◆ Standardized administration protocol in place and formalized in writing ◆ Remediation based on CBM data is embedded into Tier 1 instruction ◆ Intervention support and response linked to CBM data ◆ Trends and gaps analyzed quarterly ◆ Progress-monitoring data are shared with problem-solving team and interventionists in an organized, efficient manner	Data folders PLC minutes Sample of CBM or other progress-monitoring tool PST and SSC feedback	Initial status ___ ___ Quarter 1 status: ___ ___ Quarter 2 status: ___ ___ Quarter 3 status: ___ ___ End of year status: ___

FIGURE 5.4. Needs Assessment as a Rubric *(continued)*

Department ___ Grade Level ___	Beginning (1)	Intermediate (2)	Advanced (3)	Evidence to be provided (later, with administrative team)	Resources needed in order to improve
5. Curriculum Accessibility	◆ Syllabus neither developed nor shared ◆ In-class calendar is either not posted or rarely updated ◆ Daily agenda or expectations are not visible to students ◆ Assignments not posted to teacher web pages or other open source ◆ Assignments only available from the teacher (in person) ◆ Few, if any, materials, handouts, rubrics, and expectations are available for interventionists	◆ Syllabus shared with students at the beginning ◆ Assignment calendar posted in classroom ◆ Explicit reminders of most major assignments ◆ Due dates, late work policies, and procedure for making up missed assignments are presented to students ◆ Daily agenda or expectations are posted ◆ Some use of teacher pages to post assignments and due dates ◆ Most materials, handouts, rubrics, and expectations are available to interventionists	◆ Syllabus fully developed with clear structure, guidelines, expectations, grading practices; shared with students and parents ◆ Assignment calendar is prominently displayed in classroom and referred to frequently to keep students abreast of assignment due dates, upcoming tests and projects, etc. ◆ Explicit reminders or all major assignments ◆ Due dates, late work policies, and procedures for making up missed assignments are clearly outlined on teacher pages, class syllabi, and classroom calendars ◆ Daily agenda or expectations are posted and reflect connection to standards-based learning ◆ Regular use of teacher pages to keep stakeholders informed of curriculum pacing, due dates ◆ Nearly all materials, handouts, rubrics, and expectations are electronically available for interventionists	Updated web links Gradebook for assignments Teacher calendar printout	Initial status _____ Quarter 1 status: _____ Quarter 2 status: _____ Quarter 3 status: _____ End of year status: _____

FIGURE 5.4. Needs Assessment as a Rubric *(continued)*

Department Grade Level _____	Beginning (1)	Intermediate (2)	Advanced (3)	Evidence to be provided (later, with administrative team)	Resources needed in order to improve
6. Grading Practices	• Students are unclear about how grades are determined • Connection between learning and grades is unclear • Grades are posted in the classroom quarterly (by student ID, not name) • Grade books do not reflect current status of student performance • Grade book offers little or no usable information to PST • Lack of agreement or consistency in current grading practices • Use of zeros with means as averaging basis for grade calculation • Grading policies do not distinguish between achievement and behavior • Grades or points frequently awarded for nonacademic standards • No standards are explicitly listed in grade book • Infrequent use of rubrics • No evidence of content-specific core elements such as reading, writing, or math reflected in grading practices	• Students mostly understand how grades are determined • Connection between learning and grades is somewhat clear • Grades are posted in the classroom monthly • Most grade books reflect the current status of student performance; work turned in but not graded is noted • Grade book is helpful to interventionist as tool to support struggling students • Grade book is somewhat helpful to PST • Reviewing grading practices with action steps to move toward commonality • Reviewing use of 0 to 100 point system with alternative strategies in place for students with zeros • Behavior and achievement are evaluated separately • Grades mostly emphasize achievement and progress • At least one standards-based element is evident in the grade book • Evaluation based on rubrics most of the time • Plan is being formed so that grades reflect student proficiency in one of the core areas of reading, writing, or math	• Students understand how grades are determined • Connection between learning and grades is very clear • Grades are posted in the classroom a few times per month • All grade books are updated frequently (weekly); work turned in but not graded is noted • Grade book effectively facilitates intervention and support for struggling students • Grade book is used as part of the body of evidence in PST meetings to evaluate student achievement and to provide feedback about student progress to all stakeholders • Consistent, shared grading practices in place across PLC • Nonpunitive grading scale in place (minimum grade of 50%, incomplete option, or median score) • Behavior and achievement are evaluated separately and are standards-based • Grades focus upon achievement and progress • Standards-based grading in place for more than one element • Standardized rubrics shared, taught, and used regularly • Consistent evidence that reading, writing, and math are being evaluated based on proficiency	Grade book print-out of skill element or standard Whole grade book Weights Sample of standards-based assignment or rubric PST feedback SSC feedback	Initial status Quarter 1 status: Quarter 2 status: Quarter 3 status: End of year status:

collaboratively individualize this document further for each setting, thus fostering deeper ownership of the document and the process of RtI implementation. This would indeed be a helpful starter activity for the RtI leadership team, possibly as part of the book study or immediately following.

Evidence of current levels should be provided as well as become part of the ongoing evaluation. The results and dialogues surrounding such an assessment will allow you to prioritize needs and resources for professional development and staffing. It can also serve as a rubric, tailored to your setting, to improve fidelity of implementation across the entire building. Thus this document begins to form a bridge from implementation to evaluation and improvement of the process.

There is a place for monitoring progress in each category by an administrator (to increase fidelity). PLCs or departments would fill in the rubric, rating themselves in each category and discussing evidence with administrators to arrive at a "score" for each category. The areas of greatest concern may indicate a need for professional development or book study. It would be a rare occurrence for any PLC team to have all advanced ratings, because the bar is intentionally set high. The advanced rating indeed helps establish the target and could be used to guide improvement or action plans for departments and/or PLCs.

Looking Back through the Lens of Growth and Achievement

Depending on when schools receive final student assessment scores, schools should take time to reflect upon results. As part of this review, the principles of RtI require that we consider a student's achievement and progress as core measures of success. This is true systemically (schoolwide) for PLC teams and for individual teachers as well. Demonstrating Colorado's emphasis upon both achievement and growth, the Colorado Department of Education (CDE) has created a very helpful tool for educators (and the community) called the longitudinal growth model. Achievement is measured by proficiency on the state exam for ninth and tenth graders. The method of determining growth is significantly more complex (a student is grouped with similarly achieving peers and then growth is measured relative to this cohort), and it provides invaluable data for districts, schools, PLCs, departments, and teachers. This model also allows us to compare similar students on reading, writing, and math assessments longitudinally.

The basic premise can be demonstrated on a four-quadrant grid (Figure 5.5). The axes reflect the median for the state of Colorado for achievement (vertical axis) and for growth (horizontal axis). Schools in the upper right quadrant celebrate high achievement and high growth, and those in the lower left quadrant have hard work ahead. True longitudinal growth data cuts through all excuses and forces teams to tackle difficult questions; it also provides opportunities to celebrate authentic success.

Within departments and PLCs in our building, teams mine this data to study the health of curriculums, intervention, and instructional practice. But most importantly, they use the data to make improvements across the board. They are in fact "responding to information" in order to improve learning outcomes for students. The year 2010 was our first year looking at these data and we made immediate changes to the algebra curriculum and expanded a schoolwide writing initiative (based on below average growth results). Specifically, PLC teams are asked to provide curriculum improvement plans (by unit) that demonstrate that teams are taking time to review past units in order to improve future practice.

Looking Ahead: What the Data Can Tell Us before Students Arrive

Before the beginning of the school year, data should be brought together from a variety of sources (data triangulation). Data triangulation should consist of state testing data, benchmark data, norm referenced data, and criterion data, depending on what is available to your school or district. Gathering as much anecdotal data as possible from previous teachers (especially for the transition steps from eighth to ninth and from ninth to tenth grade) will enhance the relevance of the data. Ideally the data should be sorted by risk factors and categorized by color (red indicates the highest concern; yellow indicates the next level of concern). The process and details of this data triangulation are outlined more specifically in Chapter 7 (Figure 7.3).

Determining the cut scores (for instance, what type of score on what measure places a student in the red or yellow category?) for all the assessments and how the color-coded delineation is decided should be a collaborative process with departments and the problem-solving team. Schools can establish cut scores based upon proficiency and growth, as well as risk factors provided anecdotally by a student's former teachers. Teachers can then be provided with their "red" and "yellow" students sorted by period on the first day of staff development, before their students ever arrive at school.

FIGURE 5.5 Achievement and Growth

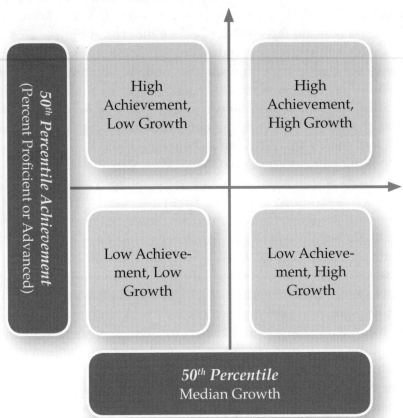

The next step is to formulate a plan for how to intervene in a preventive manner with at-risk students. This could involve the integration of McREL strategies, SIM, or other research-based interventions that are recommended for the general classroom (see Resources section). This step presents a natural opportunity for staff members who are planning to use similar intervention strategies (such as PLCs or departments) to share ideas in a professional development session led by teacher experts and administrators. Teachers should not have to wait to "get to know the students" in order to implement necessary interventions above and beyond best practices. We must be more proactive, and we have the data to make that happen. The key will be how to best utilize technology to progress monitor and track the interventions to determine effectiveness without exhausting teachers. This likely will involve curriculum-based measures (CBMs) or standards-based formative assessment for each content area (more on this in Chapters 6 through 10).

The entire plan should be part of the teacher's or department's improvement plan (professional growth plan) for the school year. The plan itself, including student samples, the teacher's grade book, and further data evidence, will be brought to the next professional development opportunity (ideally in less than one month). The entire process will help to ensure fidelity of Tier 1 instruction and interventions, one of the critical components of RtI.

At the follow-up professional development session, administrators should take the lead in collecting samples and checking over data sets and evidence to discern the measurable impact of instruction, curriculum, and interventions. Teachers should showcase exemplars for each strategy as part of the initial professional development. For students who are not making progress, staff should share in a frank discussion about how to respond. This type of trusting collaboration involves PLC groups that share ideas about what is working best in a given content or for a given type of student. If the intervention is determined to be occurring with fidelity and is still not successful for some students, the staff member should be encouraged to explore other strategies being demonstrated in other parts of the building or brainstorm solutions with the problem-solving team. As noted earlier, Rti is not a one-size-fits-all approach, and not all students will make gains from one strategy. However, the embedding of DBDM into the school's fabric offers a chance to implement a systemic process for evaluating interventions based on responsive data analysis and follow-up. The process should continue throughout the entire year as a body of interventions is implemented, data are collected, and the results are shared with colleagues and administrators. As is true with RtI in general, this process will require a robust technology and data management platform if efficiency is to be attained.

These recurring data dialogues also provide a chance for general classroom teachers to talk with members of the problem-solving team about next steps for students not responding to intervention support in the classroom. Schools can replace "staff meetings" (typically just information sharing) with these more relevant, data-driven, and meaningful Tier 1 professional development sessions.

To address the challenge of monitoring and tracking interventions, Kovaleski & Pedersen (2008) created a form to record data about teacher interventions, referred to as the Screening and Intervention Record Form (SIRF). We worked hard to avoid this type of bureaucratic paperwork initially. However, in hindsight, it would have been wise to establish some type of minimal record-keeping and data oversight from the start. Now, our resistance to bureaucracy is catching up to us because we lack careful records about what we have tried and what is working. We have to rely on anecdotal references and loosely compiled professional development documents. Though such a form is important, it demands an infrastructure of time, training, and follow-up. One such example, with some parts completed, is provided as Figure 5.6.

FIGURE 5.6. Screening and Intervention Record Form (SIRF)
Source: Modified from Kovaleski & Pedersen (2008).

Dates:
Initial Needs Assessment and Data Reflection Meeting: ___Aug 15, 2010___
Session 2: _____   Session 3: _____   End of Year _____
Subject, Grade Level, or PLC Group: ___9th Algebra PLC___

System analysis based on needs assessment and data review from end-of-year summative data
1. Given the needs assessment
   a. What particular needs are of the greatest concern for the PLC/department?
   b. How will they be addressed and what additional resources are needed?
2. Given last year's data sets
   a. As a department or PLC, review the achievement and growth matrix
      i. Any surprises?
      ii. Strengths
      iii. Areas for improvement
      iv. Action steps to address areas of improvement via instructional or curricular adjustments
      v. Resources needed
   b. As an individual teacher
      i. Were there any surprises about who made gains and who did not?
      ii. Strengths
      iii. Areas for improvement
      iv. Action steps to address areas of improvement via instructional or curricular adjustments
      v. Resources needed

Area of concern for PLC or department based on needs assessment	Goal	Resources	Metric for success with date for follow-up, who is responsible
1. Standards-based grading element	Establish essentials; choose standard to evaluate holistically	PLC time at the beginning of school year	Unit plan; Zangle grade book; PLC representative
2. Be more responsive to data during and after a unit	Set aside time to use data to make a unit improvement plan	Unit improvement plan; time during PLCs	Twice per quarter aligned with common district assessment
Need based on data review			
3. Students did poorly on geometric reasoning	Introduce geometric formulas into algebraic manipulation in first semester	Embed skills into worksheets and possibly as standards-based measure in grade book	CBM tool has some questions; evaluate homework and standard in grade book

FIGURE 5.6. Screening and Intervention Record Form (SIRF) *(continued)*

Data analysis in preparation for incoming students

3. Given the risk factors and data for current students
   a. As a department or PLC, review the gaps regarding standards and overall proficiency
      i.   Relative strengths
      ii. Areas to target
      iii. Action steps to address areas to target via instructional or curricular adjustments
      iv. Resources needed
   b. As an individual teacher, review the gaps regarding standards and overall proficiency
      i.   Relative strengths
      ii. Areas to target
      iii. Action steps to address areas to target via instructional or curricular adjustments
      iv. Resources needed

Data-based, targeted changes involving student outcomes (academic or behavioral)

Date	Target skill: Percentage of students at proficient level based on skill, benchmark, or standard	Strategies or interventions to put in place for Tier 1	Goal and actual percentage of students at proficient level based on skill, benchmark, or standard Goal = 85% by end of semester Actual %	Necessary adjustments, interventions	Follow-up review after adjustments (if any)		
Aug	Algebraic manipulation 45%	Embed strategic instruction; practice, spiral into curriculum with geometry (use CBM to measure and grade with standard)	45% to start		Check up in 4.5 weeks		
Sept			55% in 1 month	Increase practice, reinforce strategy, include daily warm-ups	Review at quarter: making progress!		
Oct			72% at quarter	Continue the warm-ups; use SSC to help with students not making gains, or CBM reviews	Review at semester exam		
...							

Embedding DBDM into Other Tiers: Establish a Rubric and Process to Evaluate Interventions

Beginning with the end in mind is not revolutionary thinking (Wiggins & McTighe, 2005). However, it is an easily ignored step in the process of developing an action plan for RtI implementation. There is so much to consider and each task appears daunting. Beginning with the end goal of a comprehensive system overhaul is all the more overwhelming.

Gathering data and using it to accurately identify and place students into interventions is the heart of solid standard treatment protocol decision-making. It cannot stop there, however. There is a need to measure progress, growth, and ultimately achievement as the elements that must determine the effectiveness of intervention classes. Once more, this demands a robust technology and data management platform. Each intervention must be clarified as to its

- ◆ criterion for placement
- ◆ specific description of remediation and support
- ◆ metric used to measure effectiveness (monitor progress)
- ◆ gains expected, a schedule of review dates, and persons responsible (this can be developed with contributions from PLCs or differentiated professional development, as mentioned earlier in the chapter).

The rubric for evaluation must have clear guidelines and expectations with tasks assigned and times established for frequent checks. The RtI leadership team should be tasked with monitoring the effectiveness of each intervention as well as the core curriculum and then openly sharing this information with the staff to guide professional development.

On a systemic level, if the intervention is not working for a large portion of students or for particular demographics of students, the intervention itself must be reexamined by the RtI leadership team or department in order to move the intervention in a more effective direction. In particular, assuming most students are progressing, if the standard treatment protocol intervention is not helping a student progress toward proficiency on standards, a more in-depth problem-solving approach must be applied to modify the intervention or select another. Ultimately, the goal is more effective and efficient delivery of support to students, and data will be the means to identify problems, craft solutions, and apply changes.

DBDM   One such rubric of expectations for intervention-based classes follows (Figure 5.7 on page 62). It includes a literacy, math, and behavior example, as well as the student support center. This is a data collection document, though it should be used in a dynamic way to

FIGURE 5.7. Rubric for Evaluating Tiered Interventions

Intervention (with placement criteria)	Area & tier	Assessment tool	Evaluation time (frequency)	Who is responsible	Criteria for success	Current level and target	Measure 1	Measure 2	Measure 3
Read & Rhetoric with 180 BLOCK (below proficient in reading on state test) with supporting evidence	Literacy (Tier 2)	SRI, MAZE, writing probes (short constructed paragraphs)	Twice per month	Teacher	SRI gains of more than one year by end of year, or greater, for all students				
Mastery Algebra with Remedial Math BLOCK (below proficient on state math test—2 years behind) with supporting evidence	Math (Tier 2, 3)	CBM, MAPS, ALEKS gains	CBM every two weeks; MAPS three times per year	Teacher	Reduce gap with peers on standards-based proficiency measures and on CBMs; MAPS RIT gain of one year, for all students				
Student Support Center (Flexible; targets those below proficient across content areas) with supporting evidence	Academic and organization (Tier 1 and 2, and at times, 3)	CBMs, credits, grades, common district assessments; User surveys; Quantity analysis	Depending on assessment	SSC staff	Pass all classes, year's gain in all academic areas on benchmark tests, for all students				
Community Mentorship Program (*Ganas mentorship*) (various risk factors, including discipline, attendance, and engagement)	Behavior, attendance, and engagement (Tier 2)	Attendance, surveys, grades, credits	Depending on intensity of need, weekly up to monthly	Dean and mentor	Attend and pass all classes, no discipline issues, for all students				

provide feedback to teachers in charge of the programs. Carefully conducted data dialogues are necessary so that teachers are neither offended nor discouraged. Trust must be fostered in these potentially difficult conversations. For most educators, dealing with transparent dialogues about measurable outcomes is fairly new, and thus training will be essential.

The collaborative development and use of a rubric to measure the effectiveness of interventions will go a long way to ensuring that the use of data is driving decision-making. When teachers have ownership in the development of the target and they have the means to measure progress toward the target, improvement will become a much more intentional endeavor. Time must be allotted to review the data to determine if an intervention is effective (reviewed by RtI leadership team). Ideally, most of the data work is done electronically with modern databases and technology services. If not, the likelihood of efficient follow-up is diminished.

Evaluation and Fidelity Checks (Classroom Walk-Through)

Though the topic of teacher evaluation demands more development than this book can designate, it is worth noting its importance and some lessons learned. Is your system for staff evaluation going to meet the demands of rigorous RtI implementation and maintenance? Our early experience indicated the need to repurpose the evaluation process as a whole through the use of data. For RtI to be implemented with fidelity, data must be an integral part of the evaluation process in concert with quality feedback delivered to teachers based on class observations.

Schools may not have capacity to unilaterally enact changes to evaluation systems, but they can create classroom walk-through fidelity checklists for teacher evaluations. Such a form, collaboratively and transparently developed, should include two sections, Student Engagement and Teacher Behaviors. The guiding checklist would include the most desirable (research-based) academic and behavioral strategies that teachers can use to increase engagement, progress, and achievement. The checklist would also include a location for specific feedback and means for follow-up. In other words, is the administration observing the behaviors it is promoting as best practice? Are the themes being taught in professional development actually being implemented? When administrators increase the frequency and randomness of classroom observations, linked with specific feedback based upon measureable outcomes, the quality of instruction and fidelity of RtI implementation will strengthen.

In addition to observable teacher and student behaviors, the following classroom and assessment data should be regularly reviewed during "data days" (perhaps quarterly):

♦ Rate of student failure in the class (percentage of students with F grades)
♦ Percentage of students meeting benchmark over the course of the year (three times per year)
♦ Growth of students on progress-monitoring tools (and/or common rubric graded writing samples). Are students progressing toward standards?
♦ Comparative success of students on common assessments (across PLCs or grade levels)
♦ Professionalism of grade book (maintained regularly, standards-based elements in place)
♦ Curricular accessibility (via website, class calendar, assignments and expectations easily available to all stakeholders)

Summary of Big Ideas for Using DBDM to Improve Outcomes across Tiers

1. Share and review data from prior year to evaluate school, PLC, teachers, and students.
2. Use this data as a means to reflect on programs, interventions, curriculum, instructional integrity, and overall building health (achievement and growth matrix).
3. Share current year's data with teachers to anticipate areas of growth and concern (risk factors).
4. Build action plan for strategies and intervention support to use in the classroom.
5. Train staff on strategies and interventions and on means to monitor progress.
6. Conduct observations, review measurable outcomes of interventions and instruction, and provide specific feedback to ensure fidelity.
7. Review data after a month of the implementation of the strategy to determine effectiveness, share exemplars, and respond.
8. Keep gathering data and responding as necessary to improve learning outcomes for all students.

Schools that embrace the challenges associated with DBDM will significantly improve and eventually embrace the RtI process entirely as it becomes the vehicle for professional development.

6

Strengthen Tier 1 with Professional Development, PLCs, and Standards-Based Assessment

The danger of shortcutting (or ignoring) the enhancement of quality core instruction will usually be brought to light due to an overextended Tier 2 support system and excessive student failure rates (coupled with unsatisfactory scores on standardized exams). Though seemingly obvious and continuously preached by RtI experts as an essential first step, strengthening Tier 1 is also the easiest element to bypass on the way up the intervention ladder. Invest your time and resources (initially and ongoing) at the base of the pyramid, and all other components will be much easier to structure. This chapter will emphasize the following means to strengthen Tier 1 in high schools:

Professional development must be continuous, relevant, focused, outcomes-driven, and differentiated.

Professional learning communities must be firmly in place and continuously improving (common goals, collaborative, and data-driven).

Standards-based, transparent grading practices should be in place schoolwide and used to inform all stakeholders.

Professional Development

Because RtI continues to demand increased fidelity of instruction, professional development will become all the more important as schools seek to construct an effective tiered instruction framework. Research supports the need for "authentic, embedded and sustained professional development" with teacher coaching and modeling to increase student progress (Vaughn, Wanzek, & Fletcher, 2007). While some schools have a strong professional development infrastructure already in place, others will need to organize from the ground up. Though this can and should be a shared venture among staff and administration, the implementation and follow-through must be guided by the RtI leadership team.

Teachers often desire more coherence, and evidence suggests it can improve learning outcomes (Goodlad et al., 2004). A unified vision and clear objectives, often referred to in research literature as instructional program coherence (IPC), includes characteristics that link professional learning communities and RtI together. By definition, IPC is "a set of interrelated programs for students and staff that are guided by a common framework for curriculum, instruction, assessment and learning climate, and are pursued over a sustained period" (Newmann et al., 2001, p.299). The proposed characteristics:

1. Curriculum, instruction, assessment, and learning climates are coordinated, both within grade levels (horizontally) and across grade levels (vertically).
2. Support programs are coordinated with the school's instructional framework to support the needs of students at risk or struggling learners.
3. School organization is designed to support the implementation of this framework.
4. Materials, programs, and other resources are designed, allocated, and implemented in a manner consistent with the instructional framework (Newmann et al., 2001).

Consider how these characteristics apply directly to PLCs and to the RtI framework in general. The goal is cohesion, and it is up to the leadership team to actively promote and sustain a clear vision.

Bender and Shores (2007) note the need for more peer-oriented observation among teachers to provide an additional layer of fidelity of treatment. Further research has noted the need for the following elements to foster effective professional development:

♦ Peer coaching (Joyce & Showers, 1988)
♦ Teacher networks and study groups (Kratochwill, Volpiansky, Clements, & Ball, 2007)
♦ Informational feedback (Noell & Gansle, 2006)

All of these elements demand transparency, openness to feedback, and accountability from teachers in order to be effective. As noted in previous chapters, professionalism and trust must exceed fear and the desire to close the classroom door. For many high schools, this degree of transparency, peer coaching, and observational opportunities is best facilitated through PLCs.

Here are some potential steps for guiding professional development at the high school level:

1. Know your students.
2. Differentiate instruction and implement evidence-based strategies.
3. Measure results.
4. Continue or adjust.
5. Reflect and respond.

It is understood and explicitly demonstrated that DBDM is the means to monitor the entire professional development process.

Research-based strategies

On a holistic level, staff should have extensive training on the strategies that work best in classrooms. Some of them are part of common classroom expectations, such as scaffolding, differentiation, formative assessments, and literacy strategies like graphic organizers. Other examples are provided in Figure 6.1, starting on page 68, to address various high school needs.

Early work by Stevens and Rosenshine (1981) and Rosenshine (1997) points to the importance of using research-based teaching methods, including review, practice, scaffolding, feedback, and cognitive strategy instruction. Teaching universities commonly include these elements in training programs. Adding to this foundation, the summative work from the McREL's meta-analysis (Marzano, Gaddy, & Dean, 2000) identifies the nine instructional strategies that have the highest impact on student learning in the general classroom (Tier 1):

1. Identifying similarities and differences
2. Summarizing and note-taking
3. Reinforcing effort and providing recognition
4. Homework and practice
5. Nonlinguistic representations
6. Cooperative learning
7. Setting goals and providing feedback

FIGURE 6.1. Tier 1 Intervention Menu

Problem	Prevention Ideas	Reaction	Resource
	Effort & Organization		
Failure to complete homework (HW)	Recommend or require use of planner Random HW lottery drawings HW written on board and discussed before the last two minutes of class Increase accessibility of homework (web calendar, grade book links) Make HW more meaningful and relevant Reward completion of HW with chance to retake quiz	Quick talk Lunch contact Enrichment time Call home	Teacher
Lack of class participation	PBIS tickets recognizing positive behavior, for monthly drawings Reward participation Make it fun to participate (games, projects) Engage students with questions they can answer Use of teacher proximity Have students present solutions on board, give speeches, etc. Varied, creative participation opportunities	Quick talk Call home	Teacher Counselor Community liaison
Failure to make up work	Use of planner Verbal reminder Grade posting from Zangle in classroom Post or provide calendar of work due dates	Quick talk Lunch contact Call home or email Email counselor or high-risk liaison	Phone call Counselor Liaison Student support center
Failure to use resources (SSC, enrichment, teacher plan period)	PBIS tickets for showing up Verbal reminder Personal Invitation Post a "See the Teacher" sign-up sheet	Call home Email counselor	Teacher Phone call
Lack of perseverance (no follow-through, not turning in work)	Organization Day (clear the book bag!) Class participation contract Recommend completed work folder Verbal reminder to turn in work	Quick talk Call home	Teacher Counselor

FIGURE 6.1. Tier 1 Intervention Menu *(continued)*

Problem	Prevention Ideas	Reaction	Resource
Lack of organization	Use of planner Use of binder for each class Backpack cleanout day Use of teacher proximity Accordion folder for each subject's daily work	Help with organization Require binder system	
Skill Deficiency			
Literacy-related	Pre-teach vocabulary directly Vocabulary on board or Word Wall Visual strategies to learn words and concepts Other PLC ideas Strategies to organize information from text ILP strategies (note-taking strategies)	Get help of LRT Review McRel best practices Refer student to reading class	LRT Best practices information Counselor
Content-related	Think-alouds by teacher Thinking maps Write-to-learn activities Model problem-solving Dynamic grouping Graphic organizers Check for reasonableness PLC ideas Ask students to explain reasoning	Recommend SSC Contact counselor Enrichment time Refer student to PST team LRT	Teacher Counselor SSC PST team

FIGURE 6.1. Tier 1 Intervention Menu *(continued)*

Key questions if student is not responding to interventions:	General Preventive Strategies	General Reactive Strategies
Is the student on a 504? Is the student on an IEP? Is the student in the ELL program? Is the student on an ILP?	◆ Set clear expectations (rubrics), syllabus, unit/monthly calendars ◆ Teach organization, literacy, and reasoning ◆ Use best practices (McRel) ◆ Set learning objective for each class, post it, and refer back to it ◆ Begin with an Essential Question or Big Idea ◆ Build positive relationships (5:1 positive to negative feedback to students) ◆ Use formative assessments to gather data and inform instruction ◆ Use warm-ups to review and get initial engagement ◆ Use exit tickets to demonstrate learning (or other strategies) ◆ Use PLC-developed content delivery	◆ Quick talk with student ◆ Conference with student ◆ Call home ◆ Email counselor ◆ Lunch detention to do work ◆ Conference with parent ◆ Referral to PST team

8. Generating and testing hypotheses
9. Activating prior knowledge

We should not assume, however, that teacher preparations programs are doing enough or that all teachers are prepared to deliver high-quality classroom instruction. Oddly enough, researchers often note a persistent disconnect between what teachers know about best practices and what teachers routinely do (Kavale, 1990). This gap between research and practice is further evident in how scientifically based strategies recommended by problem-solving teams fail to be implemented with any fidelity in the classroom (Flugum and Reschly, 1994; Telzrow, McNamara, & Hollinger, 2000). One way to increase fidelity of strategy implementation without adding a cumbersome layer of extra work is to use a record form (like the SIRF in Figure 5.6) and data-based decision-making. As noted in Chapter 5, the SIRF can foster accountability within the flow of professional development. Furthermore, the use of the SIRF or a similar document can provide accountability checkpoints along the way to make sure professional development is robust and enduring. For professional development to become the engine that drives RtI, it must serve two critical functions:

1. Link research-based instructional strategies with classroom practice
2. Embed accountability into process to establish fidelity

Administrators and teacher leaders would be wise to invest time, energy, and resources into improving the use of research-based instructional strategies. Applied across content areas, these form the basis for quality Tier 1 instruction. All of them require ongoing professional development efforts and follow-up accountability measures or they will gradually fade from focus. Schools' professional development delivery must make its deliberate connections to research or it will continue to be ineffective, as researchers note the lack of transportability of research-based interventions into the classroom (Kratochwill et al., 2007). This type of investment in coherent and outcomes-based professional development targeted at Tier 1 will create the best possible results for RtI in the school. From this strong foundation, each content area will benefit from specialized training and work groups.

There are, of course, many more research-based elements that will impact student learning in a positive way, such as the Strategic Instruction Model (SIM) from Kansas University (see Resources section). Some of them are content-specific for high school disciplines and employ a variety of modalities and technologies. To learn these strategies, teachers already attend a variety of classes and conferences and thus have much to offer in cutting-edge instructional innovation. These resources must be honored and they should be viewed as a school resource. A strong RtI leadership team could help to gather, catalogue, store, and share all the great ideas available from teachers motivated to improve instruction. Most importantly, master teachers should be tapped as visionary guides to train others in the building on best practices.

Professional Learning Communities

One of the fundamental assumptions about RtI implementation is that schools will need to become more efficient with time and data in a collaborative way that focuses on learning outcomes. Many of the authors of the most up-to-date RtI guidebooks (Mellard & Johnson, 2008; Johnson et al., 2009) insist that the optimum way to make this collaborative process a reality is through professional learning communities (PLCs) (Astuto, Clark, Read, McGree, & Fernandez, 1993; Dufour & Eaker, 1998). Furthermore, research supports the ability of PLCs to improve student achievement (Hord, 1997). In our school, the entire process of implementing RtI has been made much easier because of PLCs. In fact, we have discovered they are the most powerful way to strengthen the foundation of the pyramid from the very beginning.

Figure 6.2 illustrates four essential quadrants that guide the PLC process and mirror the essence of RtI itself (Dufour, Eaker, & Dufour, 2005).

The best PLCs will benefit from a common, unified approach to maximize efficiency of resources and thus be able to move more easily to responsive data analysis. A singular focus on student learning outcomes will drive discussions. If your school has not yet created the time (perhaps through block scheduling) and dedicated the resources for PLC professional development, it is recommended that you do research on the topic and share it with building and district leadership as soon as possible (some resources are provided in the Resources section at the end of the book). PLCs offer the means by which schools can continually improve core instruction and student learning. They will promote fundamental, lasting cultural changes by shifting schools from a place for teaching into a place for learning.

However it is accomplished, schools must build capacity around high-quality best practice instruction, which will demand several key components driven by high-functioning PLCs:

♦ Aligned curriculum, utilizing principles advocated in *Understanding by Design* by Wiggins and McTighe (2005): curriculum is designed with the ends in mind, formatively assessed in a variety of ways to enhance learning

FIGURE 6.2 Professional Learning Community Process

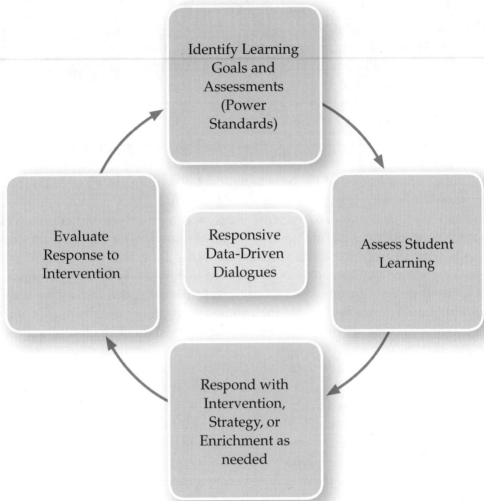

- Agreement upon power standards by which the PLC focuses energy upon those standards that deliver the greatest academic impact (Johnson et al., 2009)
- Formative, short-cycle, common assessments
- Aligned, standards-based grading policies to the greatest extent possible
- Data responsiveness that is actionable, relevant, timely, frequent, forward-looking, and reflective of the trends
- Intervention structures identified and developed
- Strategic instruction reviewed, trained, shared (Marzano, Pickering & Pollock, 2001), and nonpunitive peer evaluation structures

---

Lessons Learned

♦ Create a trusting culture for data-based discussions within PLCs with follow-up accountability in place from administration.

♦ PLCs require intensive, consistent, and ongoing training to maintain effectiveness.

One critical feature of PLCs as they dovetail with the work of RtI is that they will minimize false negatives (based on ethnic, socioeconomic status, teacher-specific, curricular concerns). False negatives are generated when a large group of students (members of a racial minority, for instance, or students who all have the same teacher) are struggling and thus individual students within that category cannot be said to have a true learning struggle because their peer group is also struggling. Minimizing this impact through careful data analysis will create the proper environment in which interventions can target the specific, genuine areas of concern for struggling students.

DBDM When we began data analysis with teachers, we initially used student grades in content classes and on common assessments (output value) coupled with standardized test scores (input value). This initial foray into DBDM demonstrated the arbitrary nature of grading practices and guided us toward the more standards-based approach represented in Figure 6.3. The data in Figure 6.3 represent a sample attempt to bring attention to teachers who are making a measurable impact upon student progress toward proficiency (while also pointing to areas that may need peer support from the PLC). The method is far from perfect, and it is not designed to harshly criticize teachers or interventionists. However, because the ultimate goal is improving learning outcomes for students and because we must measure those outcomes with data, we have to ensure that students are receiving the highest-quality instruction. This sample, based on actual data, demonstrates a few important and typical anecdotes.

According to the data in Figure 6.3, Teacher 1 began the year with a group of students nearly 10% below the average proficiency level for the PLC. Yet these students achieved above-average growth and ended the year (summative) nearly at the PLC average. On the other hand, Teacher 3 had the strongest-performing math students entering as freshmen (78% proficient compared to 60% overall entering proficiency on standards). But after one

FIGURE 6.3 Teacher and Intervention Evaluation

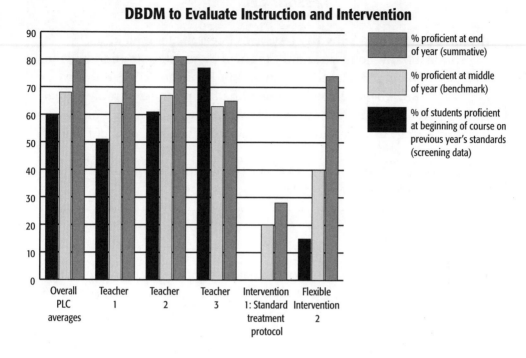

semester of instruction ("output factors"), these students were more than 15% behind their peers.

A PLC should look to Teacher 1 for guidance as to what was working well in her classroom and perhaps offer Teacher 3 the opportunity to observe other instructional strategies in other classes. These conversations and collaborative sharing of strategies do not need to be adversarial, but rather should be viewed as a positive pathway to elevate teaching practice through data-sharing and collaboration. If your school or district has an effective benchmarking assessment data platform, this process could be all the more powerful.

Standards-Based Grading and Assessment

There is certainly not enough space in this book to fully develop an argument about grading practices. However, as grades are the metric that students, parents, and often colleges are most interested in, and given that grades are a very subjective instrument to demonstrate learning, it is necessary to point out how grades fit into RtI at the high school level. Some school

> ## *Lessons Learned*
>
> **Healthy PLCs beget healthy Tier 1 systems beget meaningful RtI.**
>
> Think about who in your building will be resistant to fundamental changes involving increased accountability. In our building, the departments that have been slowest to grasp the full promise of professional learning communities (PLCs) are also the most resistant to standards-based grading, intervention delivery, accountability, and curricular accessibility.
>
> This is not ideal. Healthy PLCs beget healthy Tier 1 systems beget meaningful RtI beget improved student outcomes.

administrators, given substandard evaluation measures, are interpreting RtI to mean they must look only at Ds and Fs. This is certainly a starting point to evaluate Tier 1 instruction, but given the fact that grades are often ineffective tools to evaluate learning, schools will need to quickly deal with this difficult topic. RtI demands more of our grading systems and this entails asking teachers and administrators to look carefully at the consistency, relevance, and meaning of grades.

RtI is not a teacher's enemy, though it does demand transparency and accountability of instructional practices, student evaluation, and growth. High schools must arrive at the place where grades actually mean something, where grades are moderately consistent and transparent, and where grades tell us something relevant about student performance and provide a true picture of a student's progress toward proficiency. The longer we delay this process, the more bureaucracy teachers and administrators will have to deal with regarding RtI implementation.

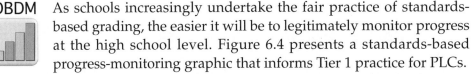 DBDM As schools increasingly undertake the fair practice of standards-based grading, the easier it will be to legitimately monitor progress at the high school level. Figure 6.4 presents a standards-based progress-monitoring graphic that informs Tier 1 practice for PLCs.

The subject matter is unspecified because it should not matter regarding the process of DBDM. All contents and subjects have standards to address and all of them can align grading and assessment frameworks to measure progress on those standards. Indeed, for RtI to really take root and blossom at the high school level, progress monitoring will need to be a mature and relevant process that is heavily reliant on standards-based grading practices.

FIGURE 6.4 Standards-Based Progress Monitoring

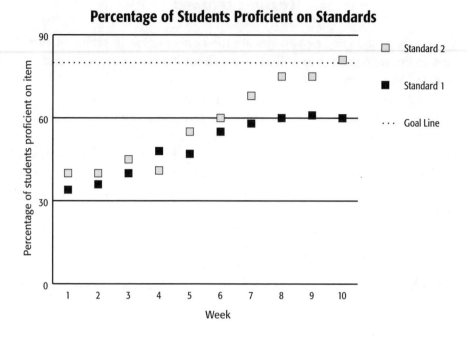

Percentage of Students Proficient on Standards

The data in Figure 6.4 show that this one particular PLC likely changed its approach regarding standard 2 and should bolster its future instructional attention upon standard 1 (flatlined). One question will face high school implementers squarely: Will our grade book system efficiently support this degree of standards-based progress monitoring without crushing teachers with extra work? I suspect many high schools will discover an antiquated grade book system in drastic need of changing or replacing.

If a teacher's grade book becomes a truer reflection of performance relative to standards (and the technology supports it accordingly), it can be used as part of the body of evidence in problem-solving team meetings (progress monitoring). Furthermore, when grading policies evolve to align with state standards, student achievement will be a truer reflection of the grade earned in a classroom; research indicates a positive relationship between alignment of instruction to standards and student achievement (Kurz, Elliot, Wehby, & Smithson, 2009). This is not meant to suggest there is a simple solution to complex problems (accountability and grading practices). Regardless of the degree of challenge, schools and districts would be wise to be vigilant and proactive on this topic. Marzano researchers (see Resources section) produce invaluable resources that can supplement professional development in the area of formative, standards-based grading and assessment.

The teacher's grade book, in the present RtI culture, will need to go through fundamental changes. Suddenly stakeholders will demand that the

Lessons Learned

Standards-based grading will elevate the conversation in schools beyond how to improve grades to a discussion about learning outcomes and targeted interventions.

I am baffled by how slowly we must move as schools and districts to create effective change. We consider our challenges in education to be greater than those in any other institution, organization, or profession and thus we need to slowly create buy-in before making systemic changes. No matter how urgent the need, we are convinced we must work gradually so as not to bruise egos and press too hard against the status quo.

Resisting this trend, one particular PLC within our school has already leaped into a standards-based grading model without looking back. After reviewing research and seeing how the practice improved the meaning of grades as well as the level of student (and parent) engagement in the learning process, these teachers did not wait around for "buy-in." This shift has already transformed our school's conversations about learning and interventions. Now students, interventionists, and teachers are talking about proficiency on targeted standards, rather than just raising a class grade.

Standards-based grading will elevate the conversation in schools beyond how to improve grades to a discussion about learning outcomes and targeted interventions. This requires systemic change, strong leadership, extensive professional development, and follow-up.

To ponder:
What limits your school or district from moving quickly in the direction of standards-based grading?

grade book be a more transparent and relevant device to inform interventionists, administrators, students, and parents. In high schools, grades for achievement and behavior are usually lumped together and the grade becomes a very ambiguous means of describing learning. The time is approaching when the high school grade book will need to differentiate how we measure performance on standards versus those "citizenship" (or workforce readiness) skills.

The following three grade book samples (Figure 6.5 on page 80) reflect different grading practices. Consider viewing these three grade books through a variety of lenses:

- ◆ Student
- ◆ Parent
- ◆ Department or PLC
- ◆ Interventionist
- ◆ Problem-solving team
- ◆ Administrator

Depending on the lens you used most actively when reviewing the three grade book samples, you probably felt a variety of emotions and considered an assortment of opinions. Which grade book conveys the greatest amount of information to parents, students, and interventionists about learning? As an interventionist, grade book C informs me about what standards the student is struggling with and what is being attempted in the classroom. Also, from a problem-solving team perspective (more on this in Chapter 7), there are effective means to measure progress as the teacher is employing a formative process to evaluate student learning. Notice also that the grading scale cuts off at 50 instead of going all the way down to zero. Putting a zero in a grade book and computing a grade by finding the mean is mathematically flawed and ethically wrong, even if this practice has been common for years (Marzano, 2010). It disproportionately punishes a student (sixfold), mostly for a behavior (noncompliance, laziness, poor attendance) that tells little about learning (though it does tell about citizenship and workforce readiness).

Look carefully at grade book A. I would argue that if your school begins to look at grade books you will find more of this type of punitive grading practice than you expect. Each time we begin discussing how to intervene with students through our problem-solving team, we pull up electronic grade books and see this type of "evidence." The student in grade book A was punished for not covering a notebook (is this *really* a high school–level English standard?) and not coming to class on time. Yet when she turned in the essay and took the test, she was "successful." The student will barely pass this class, especially because tests are not heavily weighted. Her motivation is of concern and should probably be addressed. Grades, however, for many students, are a poor motivator.

The student in grade book B may need support since he did so poorly on the test, but, again, the grade book tells little about how to target that intervention. Was he just suffering from testing anxiety (he performed sufficiently on the other material leading up to the test)? Or does he have an underlying skill deficiency that needs to be addressed? If so, would this student be given an additional chance to demonstrate mastery or is that grade fixed in stone? The grade book itself determines the structure of the intervention because it allows interventionists to respond to a failing grade. So perhaps a test is

FIGURE 6.5. Three Grade Books

Grade Book A

Assignment A= 90–100 B = 80–89 C = 70–79 D = 60–69 F = 0–59	Category	Score	Points possible	%	Comments
1. Cover notebook	Class work	0	100	0	One week to get this made up!
2. On time, ready to learn	Preparation	25	100	25	
3. Essay on book 1	Homework	85	100	85	
4. Vocabulary quiz	Quizzes	50	100	50	You should have studied!
5. Poster project	Homework	0	100	0	
6. Quarterly test	Test	80	100	80	

Grade Book B

Assignment A= 90–100 B = 80–89 C = 70–79 D = 60–69 F = 0–59	Category	Score	Points possible	%	Comments
1. Chapter 1 notes	Notes	10	10	100	
2. Chapter 1 vocabulary	Vocabulary	7	10	70	
3. Chapter 1 summary	Notes	0	10	100	
4. Chapter 1 review	Notes	15	20	75	
5. Chapter 1 test	Test	45	100	45	

Grade Book C

Assignment Advanced = 95 or 100 Proficient = 85 Partially Proficient = 75 Unsatisfactory = 65; F = 50 (lowest grade)	Category	Score	Points possible	%	Comments
1. In-class writing sample (draft 1)	Holistic writing	75	100	75	See attached rubric (follow up in 3 weeks)
2. Homework 1: Greek roots	Vocabulary	65	100	65	See attached list of words, review with note cards
3. Greek roots formative assessment #1	Vocabulary	85	100	85	Solid improvement! Note cards must have worked.
4. Finding main idea from text #1	Locating main idea	50 (original)	100	65	Need intervention: peer editing in place (replaced by test main idea #2 evidence)
5. Test 1: Use of details in writing #1	Supporting details	75	100	75	See attached rubric and incorporate recommendations
6. Test 1: Finding main idea from text #2	Locating main idea	65	100	65	Continue intervention, making progress with main idea

Lessons Learned

Some measure of a student's progress on skills or standards is a must if we expect to intervene in a targeted, strategic manner.

As a classroom teacher, I didn't concern myself much with data. I cared greatly about the class average (always hoping it would be above 70%) and grades on tests, and a bit about homework completion. Now I realize that through my grading practices, I should have focused much more on what kids were learning, not just what percentage they had in the class. Now, as an interventionist and RtI coordinator, I see how a grade book (a reflection of grading practices) can make all the difference in how a school intervenes and builds accountability. Grade books can and must be one important piece of the data puzzle regarding student achievement and progress.

A class average is essentially meaningless. Instead, teachers should look carefully at what percentage of students is failing a class because they are failing to progress toward proficiency on standards. When this number gets much above 15% for a teacher, a class, or an entire department, there are valid concerns and questions that should be discussed. What is occurring with curriculum and instruction in the classroom to promote achievement and progress?

The natural conclusion, of course, is that if teachers suspect grades are being monitored for failure rates, they will merely inflate the grades. This provides the rationale for why standards-based grading with progress monitoring and common assessments is essential to the work of both PLCs and RtI. Typically grades are subjective and arbitrary, thus an inferior metric of performance. Grades linked to performance on criterion-referenced standards make grades more meaningful to all. Some measure of a student's progress on skills or standards is a must if we expect to intervene in a targeted, strategic manner.

To ponder:

Will your school's grade books and data management system inform stakeholders about a student's progress toward proficiency?

reviewed, a retake opportunity offered, but underlying skill deficiencies may be ignored if more details are not provided.

Here are some of the benefits of switching to a standards-based assessment and grading system:

- ◆ Students, parents, and teachers gain a deeper knowledge about a student's knowledge and ability relative to standards.
- ◆ Progress monitoring is embedded in the grade book, relevant for teachers and interventionists and accessible by the problem-solving team.
- ◆ It has resulted in a significant drop in failure rates as the grading scale shifted, thus keeping more students "in the game" even after one bad unit score (the lowest score is 50%).

The seeds of standards-based grading have been planted and are spreading throughout our building, one department at a time. Schools just initiating the RtI process would save time and stress if a standards-based system were a leading priority from the beginning.

7

The Hybrid Approach: Problem-Solving Model with Standard Treatment Protocol

Two Models Blended

The RtI framework is often viewed as two basic approaches to intervene and measure responsiveness: standard treatment protocol (STP) or a problem-solving team (PST) approach (Fuchs, Mock, Morgan & Young, 2003). STP is efficient because it groups students together for research-based interventions. The PST model is more targeted, flexible, and individualized. Both rely heavily upon data. Both approaches focus on the response to intervention: define and analyze the problem, and then intervene and evaluate. Effective PST and STP structures must be continually employed to ensure that students are provided with high-quality, research-based instruction and support. More and more, schools (like ours) are finding that a hybrid model combining both approaches is most realistic for efficiency and focus (Kovaleski, 2007).

The idea that schools must choose the PST or STP approach will probably appear as a blip historically because most schools will implement both and the hybrid model will be the logical approach for RtI (Kovaleski, 2007; Barnett et al., 2004; Duhon et al., 2004; VanDerHeyden, Witt, & Naquin, 2003). The problem-solving team approach has demonstrated itself as a valuable tool in education and as the centerpiece of an RtI framework. It is considered an integral part of RtI implementation; in fact, some educators consider RtI to *be* the problem-solving process (Brown-Chidsey & Steege, 2005). Though its ability to consistently provide a disability diagnosis remains in question in the research literature, the problem-solving model is supported as a means to anticipate and prevent some learning struggles (Tilly 2003; Marston, Muyskens, Lau, & Canter, 2003; Gresham, 2002; Ysseldyke & Marston, 1999). The problem-solving process itself is not new: its basic components have been familiar in education for decades, with roots in the behavioral consultation model (Bergan, 1977; Bergan & Kratochwill, 1990).

The core elements have not changed much since Bransford and Stein (1993) described the IDEAL problem-solving method:

Identify the problem to be solved
Define the problem
Explore alternative solutions
Apply the chosen solution
Look at the effects

This acronym outlines the basic structure for Response to Intervention in general and the problem-solving model in particular.

Though research on the problem-solving process is in its infancy as part of RtI, and certainly in its ability to determine a learning disability for high school students, the anticipated benefits include the following:

◆ Facilitation of communication across contents to address multifaceted student struggles
◆ Early identification and remediation of student difficulties
◆ Selection and oversight of research-based instruction and intervention methods
◆ Reduction in over- or misidentification of learning disabilities due to inadequate instruction or cultural differences
◆ More efficient allocation of staff resources to meet the specific needs of struggling students (Gresham, 2002; Ysseldyke & Marston, 1999)

Lessons Learned

Keep your problem-solving team (PST) task-oriented and time-driven in order to focus energies on interventions and solutions.

Get students involved early and often in the process to increase likelihood of buy-in and success.

A problem-solving team is responsible for making appropriate intervention decisions for students and monitoring the effectiveness of the intervention. Successful problem-solving teams also serve as the hub of communication among stakeholders in a school to ensure that student learning plans are well understood and implemented with fidelity. In large high schools, these roles demand a high degree of organization and structure to ensure that the process is efficient and accessible.

Membership and Roles

Though this is not necessarily the case in all schools, I would recommend that the RtI leadership team and the problem-solving team be separate entities that have a different function and mission. Figure 7.1 illustrates this division explicitly.

Membership for our PST includes the Assistant Principal, counselor, school psychologist, school social worker, community liaison, dean, RtI coordinator, and special education representative as needed. More specifically, your team should include staff to fulfill the following needs (as recommended by the Colorado Department of Education's website on PST):

- ◆ Coordinator
- ◆ Consultant
- ◆ Recorder
- ◆ Timekeeper
- ◆ Parent
- ◆ Persons with expertise in
  - • Data
  - • Interventions (academic and behavioral)
  - • Parent partnerships
  - • Community resources
  - • Student participation (student involvement can increase intervention design and commitment (Reschley & Wood-Garnett, 2009)

Roles should be assigned, and a timekeeper and note-taker are essential members of the team. Timekeepers and taskmasters keep the conversations centered on student outcomes and interventions, thus minimizing inevitable tangents thatcan derail the process. The most difficult part of this process is staying focused on solutions rather than problems. Without a keen focus, teams will find it far too easy to digress and get immersed in conversations about a problem rather than the needed intervention plan and essential, ongoing review of data.

FIGURE 7.1. Roles of RtI Leadership Team and Problem-Solving Team

The RtI Leadership Team	The Problem-Solving Team
Works with school, department, and PLC data to ensure that tiered structure of instruction is of highest quality	Works with student data to screen and identify academic and behavioral difficulties ahead of time
Is in charge of professional development	Recommends specific standard treatment protocol or flexible support (like the student support center) interventions for struggling students
Ensures that Tier 1 is research-based, of highest quality, and meeting the needs of the majority of students (through data analysis)	Handles referrals from stakeholders and monitors student-level data after the initial screening and placement to make sure that struggling students are given necessary support
Handles planning, systemic implementation, and ongoing evaluation of academic and behavior tiered framework	Creates learning plans for students and communicates plans to all stakeholders
Aligns all initiatives in school under RtI to ensure instructional program coherence	Monitors student response to intervention and adjusts accordingly
Is empowered to make changes to building framework and staffing to meet needs of all students	Is versed in special education law and handles the determination of eligibility according to federal, state, and district laws and mandates
Oversees professional learning communities to ensure that they are professional, focused on student learning, and data-driven	Sets agenda and runs student-centered meetings (multidisciplinary meetings) to integrate regular education input with PST
Consists of principal and other administrators, department chairs, special educator, counselors and interventionists, data specialist, and other building leaders	Consists of counselors, special educator, school psychologist, interventionist, administrator, and general educators as needed (as well as other specialists)
Promotes data-based decision-making as the means to drive continuous improvement of all systems by monitoring all action plans	Accesses various data frequently and responds to student concerns
Communicates with entire staff and community regarding the health of all tiers of instruction	Facilitates communication among teachers, parents, and student regarding specific student plans

Eight-Step PST Process

A problem-solving team has a varied range of responsibilities, and the process itself (as outlined in Figure 7.2) relies upon several assumptions to ensure validity:

- ◆ High-quality, best-practice, research-based, Tier 1 instruction and curriculum are being delivered with fidelity (the RtI leadership team works closely with PLCs to ensure that the quality of Tier 1 is meeting the needs of a majority of students).
- ◆ Standard treatment protocol interventions are being evaluated for fidelity and effectiveness by the RtI leadership team through data and use of rubrics.
- ◆ The problem-solving team agenda is focused and time-driven to handle referrals, data triangulation, and ongoing reviews of learning plans.
- ◆ Systemic discussion about instruction and interventions are to take place primarily through the RtI leadership team.

1. Identification & 2. Placement

High schools are likely to have an assortment of Tier 2 interventions, often structured as standard treatment protocol (STP), in place for struggling students. In this model, students behind grade level are placed in some type of math or literacy support class with a fixed structure of duration, frequency, and intensity. In recent years, our school has shifted from just offering a range of STP interventions to refining the placement, instruction, remediation, and metrics by which we evaluate success for the students in the intervention. Students are placed based on needs, available space, and staff resources. The remaining students are supported through our flexible system of interventions (the student support center—more on this in Chapter 8). PSTs work closely with the RtI leadership team to ensure that students with needs are correctly identified and placed into interventions at the beginning of the school year.

To make placement decisions initially for our STP interventions, the problem-solving team works closely with middle schools and departments in our own building to formulate a student-centered plan for constructing schedules. The data loaded into this spreadsheet (see Figure 7.3 on page 90)

FIGURE 7.2 The Problem Solving Process

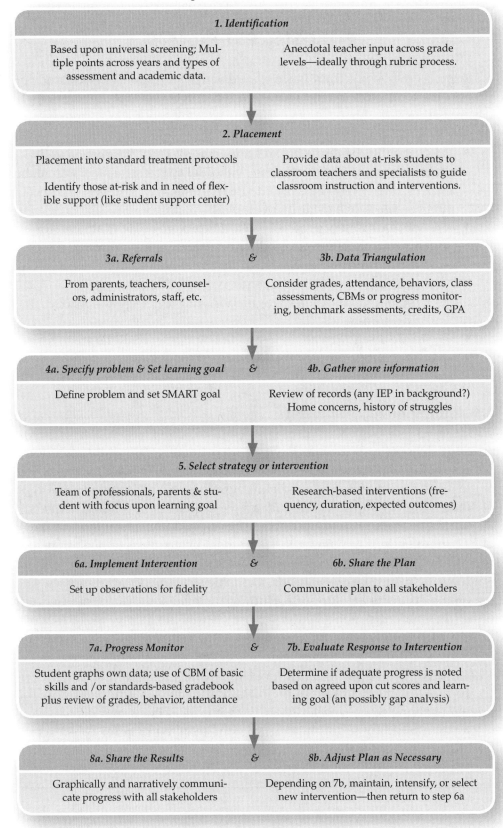

1. Identification

Based upon universal screening; Multiple points across years and types of assessment and academic data.

Anecdotal teacher input across grade levels—ideally through rubric process.

2. Placement

Placement into standard treatment protocols

Identify those at-risk and in need of flexible support (like student support center)

Provide data about at-risk students to classroom teachers and specialists to guide classroom instruction and interventions.

3a. Referrals & **3b. Data Triangulation**

From parents, teachers, counselors, administrators, staff, etc.

Consider grades, attendance, behaviors, class assessments, CBMs or progress monitoring, benchmark assessments, credits, GPA

4a. Specify problem & Set learning goal & **4b. Gather more information**

Define problem and set SMART goal

Review of records (any IEP in background?) Home concerns, history of struggles

5. Select strategy or intervention

Team of professionals, parents & student with focus upon learning goal

Research-based interventions (frequency, duration, expected outcomes)

6a. Implement Intervention & **6b. Share the Plan**

Set up observations for fidelity

Communicate plan to all stakeholders

7a. Progress Monitor & **7b. Evaluate Response to Intervention**

Student graphs own data; use of CBM of basic skills and /or standards-based gradebook plus review of grades, behavior, attendance

Determine if adequate progress is noted based on agreed upon cut scores and learning goal (an possibly gap analysis)

8a. Share the Results & **8b. Adjust Plan as Necessary**

Graphically and narratively communicate progress with all stakeholders

Depending on 7b, maintain, intensify, or select new intervention—then return to step 6a must be sorted by risk factors so most of the students at risk of failure are identified before the semester begins. Some of the identifiers are anecdotal pieces from the middle school feeders. If your school has only one feeder, you may already have this type of document in place. In our particular case, we have three major and three minor feeders so it is crucial we get a consistent picture of students to streamline our placement and risk identification process.

We send the list of student names and identification numbers to each middle school populated with only those students coming to our high school. We ask the middle school team to fill in each of the columns from "special programs" through "what interventions have been used." We then extract (through computer queries) all the existing and relevant testing data to create a comprehensive data set that enables our ninth-grade PST to carefully place students and inform teachers of potential concerns. This process is also instrumental for students transitioning from ninth to tenth grade, providing even more relevant data because we are sharing information internally about students we have had for a full school year.

These data, however, cannot capture all students. We have a separate process for students who register late or for whom we lack data (often 20% or more of our entering freshman class). Counselors or teachers administer universal screening tests (MAP survey through Northwest Evaluation Association) and interviews of students and parents to assess overall readiness before making placement decisions. The tests and interviews are short (20 minutes each) and we have the results instantly.

DBDM The anecdotal piece from teachers, quantified as a risk score, has been especially helpful and fairly innovative. Of particular interest are the recommendations for degree of intervention in different content areas and the overall at-risk-for-failure rating. Initially this database may primarily serve as a Tier 2 intervention sorting tool. Just as important is that these data be sorted by teachers so they are equipped with risk indicators on their students (besides test scores) before the semester even begins (this becomes a key component of DBDM in professional development). Teachers are then advised and coached on how to intervene (at Tier 1) with effective strategies early on (preferential seating, peer groupings, building early relationships, contacts with the family to set early tone for success, early opportunities for success offered, organization tips provided, etc.).

Figures 7.4 and 7.5 are a means to organize students based on cut scores (value at which students have been flagged for intervention support) on the state assessment for a student-centered approach to scheduling for incoming ninth graders. These tables, which contain many similar acronyms, are meant

FIGURE 7.3. Eighth-Grade Placement Spreadsheet

Student		Please indicate any special program (IEP, 504, ELL, SAIL, ILP, GT, RtI Learning Plan)	Math rec. for 9th grade: R = Reg H = Hon I = Interv	Math intervention support needed, if any No supports Tier 1 (in class) Tier 2 (strategic) Tier 3 (intensive)	English rec. for 9th grade: R = Reg H = Hon I = Interv	Literacy intervention support needed, if any No supports Tier 1 (in class) Tier 2 (strategic) Tier 3 (intensive)	Science rec. for 9th grade R = Reg H = Hon I = Interv	Overall at-risk for-failure rating. 1 = lowest 2 = low-medium 3 = high-medium 4 = highest	Please indicate what interventions have been used (s.maker, Read 180, etc.)
Name	ID	Special Programs	R,H,I Math Rec	N, 1, 2, 3 Math Support	R, H, I English Rec	N, 1, 2, 3 Lit Support	R, H, I Science Rec	1, 2, 3, 4 Risk Rating	Interventions

FIGURE 7.4. Intervention Overview

Intervention (with criteria)	Area & tier	Assessment tool	Evaluation frequency	Who is responsible	Criteria for success
Read 180 (Low in reading)	Literacy (Tier 2)	SRI	Bi-quarterly (every 4.5 weeks)	LRT, teacher, RtI action team	SRI gains of more than 1 year; MAP reading gains of more than 1 year
Mastery Algebra with MT block (Low math)	Math (Tiers II & III)	CBM; MAP; software like ALEKS	CBM every 2 weeks; MAP 3 times per year	Teacher, RtI action team	Mastery on CBM of > 50% ALGEBRA 1 avg; MAP math gain of more than 1 year
Math Tutorial (support ALGEBRA 1) (Low or low-mid in math; OK in reading)	Math (Tier 2)	CBM; MAP; Common ALGEBRA 1 district test; ALGEBRA 1 class grade	CBM every 2 weeks; MAP 3 times per year; Quarterly grade review	Teacher, RtI action team	Mastery on CBM of > 50% ALGEBRA 1 avg; MAP math gain of more than 1 year; Pass ALGEBRA 1 tests and class
HSS (mid-low for math and reading, plus other risk factors)	Organization and academic support (Tier 2)	Credits, grades	Quarter progress; weekly grade checks	Teacher, RtI action team	Earn at least 6 credits per semester

CBM = curriculum-based measures, or any form of progress monitoring tool
CSAP = Colorado Student Assessment Program
MAP = Measure of Academic Progress (nationally normed benchmark assessment)
SRI = Scholastic Reading Inventory (a basic measure of reading level)
U = unsatisfactory; PPL = partially proficient low; PP = partially proficient
LRT = literacy resource teacher (reading specialist buildingwide)
PST = problem-solving team
ALEKS = math intervention software
SSC = student support center

ALGEBRA 1 = Integrated Algebra and Geometry, our regular freshmen math offering
MT = Math Tutorial
Eng = English
PES = Physical Earth Science
PE = Physical Education
WH = World History
C.Apps = Computer Applications
SH = study hall
HSS = High School Success (guided study hall for credit)

FIGURE 7.5. Student Placement Guideline

Non-sheltered special education/ELL	Reading & Math Low/Low	R/M Low/Low-mid	R/M Low/Mid	R/M Low-mid/Low	R/M Mid/Low	R/M Low-mid/Low-mid	R/M Low-mid/Mid	R/M Mid/Low-mid	R/M Mid/Mid
Math (tier)	Mastery Algebra Double BLOCK (2, 3)	ALGEBRA 1	ALGEBRA 1	Mastery Algebra Double BLOCK (2, 3)	Mastery Algebra Double BLOCK (2, 3)	ALGEBRA 1	ALGEBRA 1	ALGEBRA 1	ALGEBRA 1
Math Support (tier)		MT (2)	SSC (1, 2)			MT (2)	SSC (1, 2)	SSC (1, 2)	SSC (1, 2)
Reading Support (tier)	R-180 plus English (2, 3)	R-180 plus English (2, 3)	R-180 plus English (2, 3)	SSC (1, 2)	SSC (1, 2)	SSC (1, 2)	SSC (1, 2)	SSC (1, 2)	SSC (1, 2)
English (tier)				Eng (with SSC 1, 2)	Eng (with SSC 1, 2)	Eng (with SSC 1, 2)	Eng (with SSC 1, 2)	Eng (with SSC 1, 2)	Eng (with SSC 1, 2)
Social Studies		WH (with SSC 1, 2)	WH (with SSC 1, 2)	WH (with SSC 1, 2)	WH (with SSC 1, 2)	WH (with SSC 1, 2)	WH (with SSC 1, 2)	WH (with SSC 1, 2)	WH (with SSC 1, 2)
Science	PES co-taught (2)	PES (with SSC 1, 2)	PES (with SSC 1, 2)	PES (with SSC 1, 2)	PES (with SSC 1, 2)	PES (with SSC 1, 2)	PES (with SSC 1, 2)	PES (with SSC support)	PES (with SSC 1, 2)
Study Hall	No study hall	No study hall	SH or HSS (2) (pending risk factor)	SH or HSS (2) (pending risk factor)	SH or HSS (2) (pending risk factor)	SH or HSS (2) (pending risk factor)	SH or HSS (2) (pending risk factor)	SH or HSS (2) (pending risk factor)	SH
Required Electives	PE or C.Apps	PE or C.Apps	PE or C.Apps	PE or C.Apps	PE or C.Apps	PE or C.Apps	PE or C.Apps	PE or C.Apps	PE or C.Apps
Elective Choice	Yes	Yes	No	No	No	No	Yes	Yes	Yes

Refer to key for Figure 7.4.

> ## *Lessons Learned*
>
> Work carefully at transition points (eighth grade to ninth, and ninth to tenth) to communicate student risk factors to all key stakeholders.

similar acronyms, are meant to be used by members of the PST, not really by a larger audience (thus the shorthand notation). Both the tables are meant to serve merely as guides, of course, for what may work in your building. Your schedule, intervention offerings, staff, resources, and assessments will vary greatly and so will your tables to organize them.

The first column of Figure 7.5 shows a schedule for a student who scored low in reading *and* math on the state test, verified through benchmark tests as well, but not with an individualized education plan (IEP) or English Language Learner (ELL) services. For the students low in both reading and math (probably less than 5 percent of students), we institute a scheduling model that emphasizes remediation of reading and math through intensive interventions (these students would not have a study hall). This type of document allows us to ensure we are able to meet the needs of all students likely to struggle (with staffing resources and flexible support).

3. Referrals & Data Triangulation

Many schools will choose to rely exclusively on referrals to the PST from teachers or parents. Though promptly handling referrals is important, it is advisable and essential to be more proactive through data analysis. We continually filter data sets in search of students who are beginning to struggle. We check D/F reports weekly and look at attendance and behavior incidents to identify emerging risk factors. We then initiate a plan of action based on this data and involve teachers and parents before either may have seen the full nature of the developing concern. This has helped our school stay ahead of the referral process almost entirely. If we wait until a parent makes a referral, it means we probably failed in our work with data triangulation to notice the problem sooner.

Inevitably, even with an effective data triangulation process in place and attentive teachers, parent referrals will arrive for students perhaps not on the radar list. Parents and guardians who sense that their child is falling behind and not receiving appropriate services will often ask that the student be tested for special education or request that the school "start the RtI process." This illustrates a fundamental misunderstanding about RtI as the instructional framework in the school rather than a consortium of interventions. My hope is that we get to a point when we will not think of RtI as something that can be put in place or taken away. RtI is always "in place" if your school is doing things correctly. Doing a better job of educating and informing parents and other stakeholders about RtI (as mentioned in Chapter 5) would certainly go a long way to avoid such misconceptions.

Ideally schools will be proactive regarding student struggles. In a perfect system, schools should be notifying parents and not the other way around, while always open to respond to family concerns. To this end, schools must include parents and students in the problem-solving team process, to maximize commitment and share ownership. The student may or may not have a disability, but through the RtI process we will be applying various scientifically based interventions with increasing intensity as needed to improve student progress. If the entire body of evidence suggests that a student is unresponsive to the research-based interventions (implemented with fidelity) and is not part of an exclusionary group (visual, hearing, or motor disability; mental retardation; emotional disturbance; cultural factors; environmental or economic disadvantage; or limited English proficiency), the PST may move to a special education label and services (requiring a gap analysis, as shown in Appendix A). This determination, however, should not be seen as the goal of the problem-solving team process. The goal should always be helping a student improve, not labeling.

4. Specify Problem & Set Learning Goal; Gather More Information

What is the nature of the problem? Be as specific as possible because the learning goal must connect to the problem. How does the student's performance compare to that of peers (locally or nationally)? This matters because the "student" struggle may actually be a "teacher" struggle or a PLC-level (curricular) concern. For the PST team, we must make sure we are working with students with genuine concerns. For *classrooms* that have a concern, the PST is not the place (consider the RtI leadership team for this task).

The goal must be SMART (Specific, Measurable, Attainable, Relevant, and Time-bound), as suggested by Conzemius & O'Neill (2001, Chapter 2), and agreed upon by the group. Once the goal is decided, the team should gather any additional information (a review of records) that may be helpful from previous settings, teachers, counselors, and so on.

5. Select Strategy or Intervention

What intervention? This clearly depends upon the individual student and the specific area of concern. As noted throughout this book (and in all RtI literature), the intervention must be research-based (evidence-based or scientifically based). It must be practical, age-appropriate, and timely if it is to be successful. Furthermore, it must connect to the learning goal for the student. The student should have a say in the selection process, as the student ultimately will determine its success.

The Resources section of this book will lead your PST to various intervention sources (including the *Pre-Referral Intervention Manual*, McCarrey and Wunderlich, 2006), though the team is likely to already have some interventions to select from. Some may be STP options, where students are placed into an intervention of fixed duration and protocol. Others require a more flexible approach by teachers and, in our case, interventionists in the student support center. A PST should have a database of options for a variety of possible student struggles that are research-based, practical, and proven with students (and with staff that can implement them with fidelity). Some schools choose to designate an intervention team to organize and sort intervention options. For some schools, just working from an evaluation rubric will bring the most usable intervention options to the attention of the PST.

6. Implement Intervention & Share the Plan

The intervention must be implemented with fidelity (agreed-upon frequency, duration, and intensity). The fidelity will need to be monitored through professional development and data evaluations, as mentioned throughout the previous chapters. Once a plan is developed, it should be shared with all team members (including parent and student). One sample template of a rudimentary plan follows (Figure 7.6). It should be considered as a dynamic document to track any and all interventions attempted with a student at all tiers. For many schools, this form may be electronic and part of a comprehensive data management system.

7. Progress Monitor & Evaluate Response to Intervention

How will we know if a student has responded to the intervention? One approach is to determine a gap analysis and establish a goal line (see

FIGURE 7.6. PST Template for Student Learning Plan

Name: _____

Grade: _____   Date: _____

Student Strengths:

Area of Concern: State general area of concern or need.

Present Level of Performance: State the current ability level of student relative to the area of concern and relative to peers and/or national norms.

Learning Goal: Include measurable, specific learning target and how it will be measured, by whom, and how often.

Intervention Plan: Include the selected, approved, research-based intervention, grouping, duration, frequency, and intensity.

Intervention Review: Who is responsible for follow-up? Provide evidence regarding effectiveness of intervention.

Appendix A) to calculate just how great a gain is needed to catch up with peers on a given skill. Another measure is the rate of improvement (or growth). This is a measure of the slope of the line (steep is good, flat is indicative of a nonresponse). To a large extent, schools will need to rely on professional judgment and follow the guidelines established by the district or state or utilize protocols recommended by national organizations. Furthermore, RtI must form only part of the body of evidence of a student's progress and achievement. Some guidelines offer the following suggestions, as supported by our school district and others across the nation (Colorado's model is presented as Appendix A):

- At least four data points at Tier 1 would be needed to make a referral to Tier 2 interventions.
- Tier 2 monitoring should occur twice per month. If four to six data points are below the goal line, change or supplement the intervention.
- If three or four interventions have not increased the slope for a student toward the goal line, then the PST will need to intensify the intervention up to and including Tier 3.
- At Tier 3, progress is monitored more frequently (weekly) on nationally normed progress monitoring tools. If four to six data points are below the goal line, intensify or add interventions and consider special education eligibility (depending upon the state)

In general, when we are looking at a student's response to intervention, we look at a body of evidence and the specifics of the learning plan. That is why graphing a student's data can be important as a visual tool to demonstrate responsiveness (see Figure 7.7 and Figure 7.8). Ultimately we are trying to determine if the intervention is working for a given student. To do this effectively, as emphasized throughout RtI research, we must ensure the intervention itself was targeted to improve the particular area of concern for the student; scientifically based, evidence-based, or research-based; and implemented with fidelity. For some goals, like attendance, assignment completion, and behavior, national norms may not be important. For other areas, we may need more targeted goals. Here are some possible and practical goals and metrics for the high school level:

- Improve the number of correct responses on pre-algebra CBM (like the MCAP2 by AIMSweb) administered to all algebra students (includes integers, order of operations, graphing, number sense, linear patters, multiple representation of functions).

- ◆ Improve reading according to the Scholastic Reading Inventory (SRI) administered via computer
- ◆ Improve writing based on rubric-graded writing sample (grammar, structure, details, etc.)
- ◆ Improve reading comprehension as measured by MAZE probes through AIMSweb
- ◆ Holistic approach to standards-based assessment: are students making progress toward an established benchmark? This method has been of particular benefit for math and English interventions and will likely form the foundation for RtI in the future.

Other items should also be considered for measuring, such as basic arithmetic, spelling, and oral reading fluency probes. However, we have found these to be the most impractical for the high school setting (though perhaps relevant for students already diagnosed with disabilities).

Many schools will make a flow chart of the following questions the PST should consider before making any adjustments to the student's learning plan:

- ◆ Is the student making progress toward benchmark?
    - • if yes, maintain intervention
    - • if no, verify fidelity of treatment and/or select new intervention option
- ◆ Is the progress sufficient to allow the student to catch up (reduce the gap with peers)?
    - • If yes, maintain intervention
    - • If no, increase intensity or select different intervention
- ◆ Are more interventions needed to help the student catch up?
    - • If yes, increase intensity of intervention or layer additional support
- ◆ Is the gap with peers too large to realistically shrink in one school year?
    - • If yes, work closely with special education department and ramp up intensity of interventions. A more comprehensive assessment may be necessary to determine if the student has a disability.

8. Share the Results & Adjust Plan as Necessary

The federal law regarding SLD is clear that parents must be notified about individualized assessments and notification forms must be signed. Once a PST suspects that a student has a disability, the team must move fairly quickly and transparently so that services are not withheld. Though determining a disability is not the primary purpose of the PST (nor RtI in general), parents must be involved throughout the process and movements across tiers. Data should be shared and discussed to make sure the process is outcomes-based and student-focused. If results are not as expected, adjustments must be made so as not to waste time.

Tracking Forms

From the start, we recognized the difficulty of maintaining a system for keeping track of students in the various tiers across our high school. Developing a process to track students in the various tiers, given our data management system, has turned out to be very challenging. Our district has experimented with a variety of software interface programs for managing RtI learning plans, none of which has been ideal. For this reason, our PST supplements the district system with a spreadsheet for all the tracking components and individual entry fields required to effectively keep tabs on students at various tiers.

The data you will need to track, for increased efficiency, includes the following:

◆ Basic demographics and testing information on student
◆ Area of academic or behavioral concern
◆ Present level of performance

Lessons Learned

At our high school, we had an initial rollout of our problem-solving team for the ninth grade and then relied on our counselors and teachers to handle referrals for other grades in a piecemeal way. Though there was sound logic behind starting in ninth grade, we were a bit too slow in developing a more systematic and protocol-driven approach to the upper grade levels. And this, to our dismay, is where we have seen the bulk of referrals for special education testing. We were not fully prepared. Thus it is advisable to train many more teams on the PST model at the outset to avoid the surprises sure to come your way if you have not laid the groundwork. Once parents become educated about the RtI process, referrals and requests about services at all grade levels will increase whether the school is ready or not.

   ◆ Learning goal
   ◆ Intervention plan (including frequency, duration, who is responsible)
   ◆ Intervention review (when, who, evidence, response plan)
   ◆ Achievement and growth data about a student's performance

The challenges begin when students need multiple interventions. This means multiple entries into a database that quickly becomes overwhelming and difficult to sort. Ideally, your school district will invest in a high-quality data management system that aligns RtI learning plans with all databases (including teacher grade books) and that connects to individual education plans (IEPs) for special education.

   As mentioned previously in the chapter, forms do not create a system but rather support it. Often we assume that if we have forms, we have a system. A system is a *means* for the forms to document the work of the team, in a comprehensive, sortable, and cohesive manner. Otherwise, forms become pieces of a bureaucracy that merely help us to store information. A system is the process that allows us to respond to the information and make meaningful decisions because the student information is readily available at our fingertips. Don't let the forms dictate the process. *The process must dictate the forms.*

Case Studies

Case Study 1: "Paul"

Student Background: "Paul" was a tenth-grade regular education student with average scores for math and reading. However, he had struggled with writing since his seventh-grade year (based on teacher feedback and scores on state writing tests). Paul disliked to write and was fairly resistant to any intervention support to address this area.

   In the social studies class (U.S. History), all sophomores are given a common writing probe every month that is graded holistically on a rubric. The ultimate goal is for students to reach a proficient level of writing on this probe (different topic, same expected length and evaluated the same way each time via the rubric) by the middle of the second semester (about month 7).

DBDM   On the baseline writing sample, Paul scored a 1 while the average score for all sophomores was 2.5 (see Figure 7.7). Given this gap with his peers, the classroom teacher worked in a more targeted way with this student when students were all given a chance to revise and correct the first writing probe, referred to as Intervention (Int) 1 in

FIGURE 7.7 RtI for Paul (Writing)

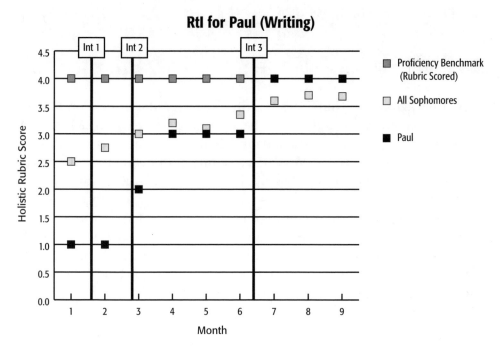

figure 7.7. The next probe showed no real progress, though other students did make gains with the Tier 1 classroom support and feedback.

Given these data (including the body of evidence suggesting past writing struggles), the problem-solving team recommended pulling Paul from study hall so he could get specific feedback on writing from a literacy specialist in our school (referred to as the LRT). The result of this targeted feedback (use of the rubric, think-alouds, explicit example) was promising, as the student improved on the next writing sample (after Int 2 in Figure 7.7). Though he was a bit resistant to the support, he cooperated once a goal was defined and respect established.

Paul continued to progress thanks to quick feedback sessions with the LRT (Tier 2) and the classroom teacher (Tier 1). However, once he reached a score of 3 on the rubric, he stalled out and seemed complacent. The PST was notified and a discussion ensued about what the student was truly capable of. Was a 3 good enough for this particular student? How do we best utilize our limited resources? Are there students more in need of help to even get to a score of 2? The LRT, who had established a strong working relationship with Paul, wanted to intensify the support to challenge him further.

The LRT worked more closely with Paul on several in-class writing assignments to provide editing and revision support, including chances for him to reciprocate the feedback to the LRT and his peers (referred to as Int 3 in Figure 7.7). The effort paid off: Paul reached a proficiency score and maintained it for the rest of the school year.

Case Study 2: "Kim"

Student Background: "Kim" was a ninth-grade regular education student. Data from eighth grade and further back showed a persistent lack of proficiency in reading, writing, and mathematics. Math was her lowest nationally normed score on the NWEA MAP (consistently at or below the 12th percentile). Kim had passed her middle school classes and received math and reading interventions. As her math scores were not in the lowest category, she was not placed in our math tutorial program but instead referred to our student support center (see Chapter 8 for more details on the SSC). Kim was also placed in a guided study hall (earning an elective credit) where we would have access to her for math and language arts support (on a flexible, rotating schedule). In Figure 7.8 this is referred to as Int 1.

Additional screening data from our math curriculum-based measure (CBM) tool, administered in the first three days of school as a baseline for progress monitoring (example in Appendix C), placed Kim in the lowest 5th percentile of her peer group, including students with disabilities and English language learners. We intensified tutoring support immediately so Kim could work on the pre-algebra skills featured on the CBM, all as part of the first intervention in the student support center.

Frequency and focus of intervention: A full-time math teacher who runs the student support center worked with Kim in small-group tutoring sessions (1:3) for skill remediation, including repetition, and strategy instruction. The sessions lasted for thirty-five minutes twice a week. Kim was also assisted with algebra homework and preparation for tests and quizzes.

Evaluation of RtI: The follow-up progress-monitoring CBMs, administered every two weeks after the baseline, showed gains for most students who received similar interventions, but Kim made no such gains. The first quiz in the algebra class confirmed her struggles as she lagged far behind her peers on the formative assessment as well. The problem-solving team decided to increase and adjust the intervention intensity (indicated by Int 2 in Figure 7.8).

DBDM **Increased intervention and monitored results:** The math teacher in the SSC re-taught the essential materials from the formative quiz to a small group of students, including Kim, during each study hall. The re-teaching session followed the pedagogy agreed upon by the

FIGURE 7.8 RtI for Kim (Math)

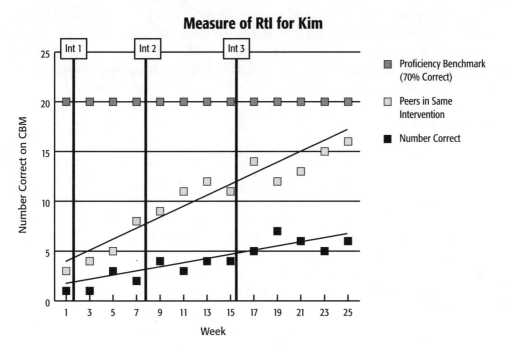

math PLC. The following day, students were all given a chance to retake a similarly formatted quiz to demonstrate mastery of the essential material from the quiz. All the students showed significant gains that surpassed mastery (85%) after dismal scores on the original quiz—except Kim. Even with the explicit re-teaching and practice, Kim made minimal gains and showed very little retention of what she had learned two days before.

Kim then began to receive even smaller-group instruction on pre-algebraic skills to help her grasp the general Tier 1 curriculum. This added degree of intervention did increase the slope of her growth line, but she was not shrinking the gap with her peers quickly enough to catch up before the end of the school year. In fact, she was falling further behind.

The data illustrate that Kim failed to respond to interventions. Math was not just hard for her; she was not demonstrating learning or retention at all. This caused concern and we decided to increase the layers of additional supports and gather more data. We saw more of Kim in the SSC and she began to do a remedial math software program (Successmaker) after school three times per week (referred to as Int 3). Her math teacher began to modify her grade by deemphasizing the weights of the tests and placing more grade emphasis upon class work and effort.

While her progress-monitoring scores showed a relatively flat response, her classroom common assessment scores (with re-teaching and retesting) were still far below the entire ninth-grade math PLC averages. We began one-on-one tutoring support in place of the software program. What became abundantly clear was that it would take too much math support (and thus no time for other necessary supports for language arts) for Kim to be successful. We placed her into the algebra 1 supplemental support class, Math Tutorial (see Chapter 9), for the second semester and focused more strategically upon remediation. She was much happier and all her grades improved, though her performance in math class continued to be of concern.

During this entire intervention phase, Kim's regular math teacher was informed and involved. Trying various classroom strategies, he changed her seat, scaffolded assignments more intently, and grouped her with a high-achieving math student in class to model strategic thinking. These attempts, however, had little to no impact on tests and CBM results. Of note, all of these interventions occurred within the first few months of school. And this particular student had stellar attendance, a willing attitude, and supportive parents, three assets that simplified the entire process.

Kim was an active part of our problem-solving team discussions based on the screening (CBM) data and her failure to respond to the interventions offered. The special education teacher on the team pulled her file and the counselor contacted the middle school to form a more complete picture. Kim had been tested for a learning disability on several occasions, dating back to second grade and most recently in seventh grade, before the RtI model replaced the IQ discrepancy formula. She never qualified, though she was very close each time. The common finding was: "She is a slow learner." In student and parent interviews, Kim and her family shared the concern that math had always been hard for her.

We worked closely with our special education department as well throughout this process because of some early concerns about Kim. Our district interpreted the state mandate to mean that we must have six consecutive data points at or below the 12th percentile on a nationally normed assessment in the presence of research-based interventions. Our in-house-developed CBM (see Appendix C) was relevant to instruction and intervention but not nationally normed. The AIMSweb probe was neither age-appropriate nor relevant to instruction but was nationally normed (these tools have improved greatly since this first case; see Resources section). Thus we used both measures (our school psychologist and a special education teacher administered these during the guided study hall) plus the MAP tests and our own state assessment (CSAP) to produce a body of evidence to suggest that Kim had a specific learning disability in math.

After the label, Kim's school day did not change. As she had been receiving increasing degrees of support throughout the year, ultimately she was receiving special education services (Tier 3) before the arrival of the label. For the following year, however, her schedule included a modified intervention algebra course mostly reserved for special education students, co-taught by regular and special educators, with built-in remediation.

Case Study 2 Analysis

Kim was our first case to move through the entire process of SLD labeling and thus it took nearly nine months (other schools across the nation are expressing similar results). Given this lengthy process, the following points were critically important:

- ◆ Parent support
- ◆ Student engagement (attendance and attitude)
- ◆ Active involvement of PST, including special educator, school psychologist, insistent math interventionist, and cooperative general education math teacher
- ◆ Some special education services, including modifications, that were in place along the way and were not being withheld pending the labeling
- ◆ Progress monitoring that was connected to classroom material
- ◆ Availability of a flexible support (student support center) and a standard treatment protocol (Math Tutorial) along a continuum of math interventions

As the first high school in our area to use RtI for determining a SLD in math, we were very uncertain of our approach. We all longed for the simpler (and quicker) days of the discrepancy model, which produced a cut-and-dried formula. However, this means of determining eligibility, applied in earlier grades, had shown that Kim was close to qualifying, but not quite. Though many members of the PST suspected a disability from very early on with Kim, our focus was upon putting interventions in place that would help her be successful. Supporting her was the focus, not the label. That made the long process well worth it. Furthermore, what is the hurry for a label anyway? If ultimately we are interested in wrapping supports around struggling students regardless of label, why would we rush into labeling a student before observing if a different set of instructional options could help her be successful?

Other Case Study Types

Most of the other cases referred to our PST resulted in students making progress thanks to an intervention. Their progress was noted in progress-monitoring tools, improved attendance, assignment completion, or on content-level or benchmark assessments.

Other cases referred to our PST were more difficult to handle. For instance, we encountered certain common stumbling blocks when dealing with struggling students:

- Parental refusal of intervention support (including ELL and IEP services)
- Students who had excessive absences and thus we had a lack of intervention access and data
- Students who resisted intervention because of stigma traditionally attached to high school adolescents who feel singled out or "dumb"
- Doubling up interventions for needy students usually required that the student sacrifice an elective class (not always a popular option)

Though we have many supports in place for organization, study skills, reading, and math (and to a lesser extent, writing), we have struggled to deal with the following groups of students, even though we have a schoolwide positive behavior support (PBIS) system in place.

- Completely apathetic students
- Students who earn solid test scores (gifted or otherwise) but are unmotivated to do the daily work necessary to pass classes. Though our RtI framework has potential to help low motivated and gifted and talented (G/T) students, this is indeed a group that schools may find challenging to support with intervention resources.
- Students with poor attendance or behavior problems (including gang activity, use of drugs and alcohol, and fighting). Though our PBIS structure has been in place for five years, some students are resistant to being in school and complying. For many in this group, our priority often shifted from intervention into a conversation about "rightness of fit" and alternate settings (including our own night school program) that would increase the likelihood of graduation. For some students in this group, we offered a community mentorship and a built-into-the-day credit recovery program (Nova Net) in our student support center. This program was very successful and will be expanded in the years to come.

Upon the framework recommended throughout the previous chapters, Chapter 8 will describe in detail how to begin plans for a student support center

(SSC) early in the RtI process so you can tailor it to your specific needs and staffing options. The following chapters will summarize our SSC journey, growing pains and all, in developing a highly functioning center geared toward flexibly supporting math and literacy at the high school level as an integral complement to all other RtI components.

8

The Student Support Center as the Hub of Flexible Intervention Delivery

High schools have struggled with RtI for a variety of reasons (see Chapter 3), many of which can be addressed through the implementation of a student support center (SSC). For instance, Shores & Chester (2009) press high schools to create a flexible system to address both basic skills concerns and content-specific deficiencies. They also note the benefits of schools offering credit recovery, virtual classroom offerings, and extended day or school year. The problem with expecting students to be available for extended day or year is that many students are resistant to intervention and too busy (Sugai, 2004). If reaching struggling students is ultimately the goal, high schools would be wise to find the means to implement interventions *inside the school day*, not outside of it.

Furthermore, high school interventions face the daunting task of targeting both content-level support (for credits) and remediation skills to empower students to reduce the gap with peers. Indeed, several researchers have cautioned high schools against abandoning basic skills in favor of merely compensating and content tutoring because this approach has not been successful for significantly struggling students (Kovaleski, 2007; Kavale, 1990; Reschly & Ysseldyke, 2002). Given various scheduling and staffing constraints, this demand upon high schools to provide such a varied set of interventions can feel daunting and unrealistic. However, to efficiently improve outcomes, high schools must find the means to flexibly deliver interventions to help *all* students improve.

FIGURE 8.1. How SSC Addresses High School RtI Concerns

Area of High School Concern	*How the Student Support Center Facilitates Tiered Interventions*
Changes in organizational structure (Sugai, 2004): High schools offer less individual attention than elementary schools and therefore at-risk students go undetected more easily.	SSC provides individualized, flexible attention as a preventive means to reach struggling students.
Shift in academic focus (Sugai, 2004; Shores & Chester 2009): High schools move beyond skills into application, beyond supportive learning into independent learning across several contents, assuming self-monitoring, motivation, and a grasp of basic skills	SSC works with students to build independence (acts as a bridge) and also teaches self-monitoring. SSC offers both basic skills support and content-level support for math and literacy.
Nonschool responsibilities (Sugai 2004): Teenagers are working, dating, driving, and are more distracted than elementary age students; thus they have less time for interventions outside the school day	SSC offers academic and organizational supports *during the school day* to honor the busy lives of students.
Staff capacity (HSTII, 2010): Schools must build in time to collaborate and continually learn RtI and data-based decision models. Schools need flexible approaches to offer evidence-based interventions across grade levels (Kovaleski, 2007).	SSC, by having content-level teachers assist, presents increased articulation (vertically, horizontally, and across disciplines) as well as an emphasis upon progress monitoring and standards-based data to guide the intervention.
Scheduling (HSTII, 2010): Schools face the inherent complexities of high school scheduling regarding tiered interventions.	Use of open period, flexible intervention credit-based courses and credit recovery modules, study hall, and guided study hall facilitates access to students across tiers.
Resources (HSTII, 2010): Resource allocation for RtI is difficult.	SSC maximizes/centralizes staff expertise (duty hours) and intervention efficiency.
Fidelity (HSTII, 2010; Fuchs & Fuchs, 2006; Shores & Chester, 2009; National Dissemination Center for Children with Disabilities): Monitoring of instruction and intervention is a significant challenge.	By default, SSC has open access to classroom curriculum and instruction practices, fostering open and frank discussion about best practices across domains.

The student support center offers a means to answer these challenges head-on. The supports it offers are

- ◆ focused on improving proficiency on standards in reading, writing, and math
- ◆ supportive of access skills that support learning (study skills, organization, motivation, etc.)
- ◆ preventive, responsive, and targeted based on data
- ◆ flexible based on variable demand and ongoing data collection
- ◆ relevant based on critical collaboration with classroom teachers

The student support center also has the capacity to address several other areas of concern for high schools (Figure 8.1).

While addressing many needs of high schools regarding RtI, the SSC can help make instruction, curriculum, and interventions more transparent and accountable. Though this book will not cover all the details of the development and maintenance of the SSC, the following elements will be covered in some detail:

a. Evolving goals and improved outcomes
b. Requirements, resources, and physical environment
c. Selecting, accessing, and monitoring students
d. Peer tutors (training and evaluation)
e. Collaboration

Evolution of Student Support Center Intervention

The nature of our own SSC has been continuously evolving to meet the changing needs of students. This evolution is reflected in Figure 8.2 on pages 112–114 and will be noted throughout this chapter.

Our primary goal in the SSC, from the outset, has been to improve the graduation rate trend. Based on research, the best way to accomplish this goal is to focus energy at the freshman level on English and algebra because passing both courses has been shown to be a positive predictor of graduation (Christenson et al., 2008; Jimerson, Reschly, & Hess, 2008). As the SSC continues to reduce freshman and sophomore failure rates (especially in math and English), we expect the positive graduation trend noted in Chapter 1 to continue and improve for our high school, even as our demographics change.

At the outset, we believed that the student support center represented a Tier 2 intervention. However, because we mostly focused on content-level

FIGURE 8.2. Evolving Goals and Improved Outcomes: The Use of Data-Based Decision-Making in Our Student Support Center

	First Year	Second Year	Third Year
Primary Objectives	Reduce freshman failure rate Respond flexibly and efficiently to changing demographic needs	Increase remediation for mathematics and writing to sophomores Continue with first-year goals	Reduce sophomore failure rate Increase partnerships with PLCs for standards-based grading Extend support to juniors in mathematics and English to reduce failure rate and to improve ACT outcomes Continue with first two years' goals
Action Steps	Provided homework assistance Guided reading (explicit instruction about main idea, etc.) Assisted with research projects Edited written work (feedback) Provided support for test preparation Re-taught students who failed a test Taught organization and time management skills and assisted with general transition to high school Helped build work ethic (work completion)	Initiated duty hours for teachers Increased use of CBM to remediate skill deficiencies Offered computer-based credit recovery option for credit-deficient sophomores and juniors Collaborated with at-risk coordinators, deans, and assistant principal to track down students with attendance problems more efficiently Assisted teachers with web-based calendars to increase curricular accessibility	Added 10th-grade study hall to reach struggling sophomores Solidified the algebra CBM as a means of monitoring progress and informing instruction across all tiers Worked with standards-based system for algebra and English, including common writing rubric and subsequent remediation Provided ACT study sessions to juniors for math and English Provided more feedback to peer coaches via rubric of expectations Enhanced pull lists for math students reflecting performance on CBMs and classroom grades, in addition to all standardized assessment data

FIGURE 8.2. Evolving Goals and Improved Outcomes: The Use of Data-Based Decision-Making in Our Student Support Center (*continued*)

	First Year	*Second Year*	*Third Year*
Outcomes	Significant reduction in freshman failure rate (especially in English and math) after years of an upward trend Significant and positive impact on credits for the most at-risk students in the school	Continued reduction in freshman failure rate Longitudinal gains above school and state median in mathematics	Dramatic reduction in sophomore failure rate and continued reduction in freshman failure rate
Challenges	Organizing pull lists Curricular access was not efficient for all content areas Building relationships and buy-in with freshmen Dealing with arbitrary nature of grade books across PLCs and content areas Tracking down students with attendance problems, significant apathy, and lack of engagement Providing language arts and math support to students with double deficiency	Collaborating with so many teachers in the school Lack of access to struggling sophomores Several students across grade levels needed more math support than the SSC could reasonably provide Students did not readily respond to CBM remediation (no real link to classroom grade)	Our walk-ins continue to increase as a diverse population of students feel comfortable getting support—it's hard to help all those that seek support on their own (including upper classmen who have built relationships with us) Need for tighter controls for freshmen coming with passes to the SSC (more accountability)

FIGURE 8.2. Evolving Goals and Improved Outcomes: The Use of Data-Based Decision-Making in Our Student Support Center *(continued)*

	First Year	Second Year	Third Year
Unexpected Benefits	Increased schoolwide dialogue about grading practices Honors and IB students received advanced support Encouraged formative assessment principles because students could receive re-teaching support more efficiently	Vertical articulation increased as teachers worked together in SSC and reviewed curriculum Dialogue on grading continued with emphasis on standards-based grading Maturation of peer coaches, many of whom now want to be teachers	Students find it impossible to "hide" in our system. We know of and are attempting to support *every* struggling student in our building. Increased collaboration across disciplines occurs because teachers work together in the SSC Great support for students who have been absent, or to students who have joined our school late in the school year Improvements in grading systems—more standards and formative assessments to guide and inform tiered intervention delivery
Usage Data	42% of 1,840 enrolled students visited the SSC (8% get almost daily support). 9000 total visits.	43% of 1,850 enrolled students visited the SSC (11% get almost daily support). 8,400 total visits.	To be determined, but numbers are similar to previous years

support (grades, homework completion), it became clear we were mostly doing the work of Tier 1, for two main reasons: our target was on grades (reducing credit deficiency), and the traditional grading practices at Tier 1 meant we did not have many avenues for skill development or flexible remediation.

As evidenced in Figure 8.2, we have worked diligently to transform the model to include Tier 2 support as our school increases its focus upon classroom instruction and standards-based grading to enhance our Tier 1 structure. The current iteration of the SSC has applied more Tier 2–type principles that integrate more teacher support and collaboration. Allowing the student support center to grow and evolve, specialize and be flexible, has been a critical part of its success.

The reason behind showing our evolving process and goals is to encourage other schools to start small and expand the student support center. We could not have started with standards-based remediation because our school was not ready for that transition. All the changes have occurred organically, symbiotically, and gradually. Additionally, it takes time to get organized and to discover the obstacles and challenges that prevent efficiency. The more flexible and responsive schools shape the SSC to be, the more open the entire school will be to maximize this powerful intervention structure.

Requirements and Resources

Once the need is established through the use of data (more students need flexible service than the school is able to provide through standard treatment protocol interventions), the RtI team must begin to establish a resource plan. The effective delivery of SSC services requires two full-time teachers for a school with between 800 and 1400 freshmen and sophomores. Here are some staff characteristics worth pursuing:

- ◆ Both teachers should be experienced with at-risk youth, skilled with relationship building (with staff, administrators and students), knowledgeable and involved with RtI and Problem Solving Team process
  - Math teacher with special education training and skilled with data analysis
  - Language arts teacher or reading specialist with extensive experience and foundation in reading interventions; cross-content knowledge

◆ A part-time education assistant to assist with record-keeping and data processing. In our system this paraprofessional acts as a book-keeper and data entry specialist, along with performing daily bureau-cracy tasks. Depending on your SSC's expected volume and usage, this data processor may or may not be necessary in your setting.

This is not to say your staffing allocation will exactly match these descrip-tions. What will most benefit your student support center will be two teach-ers (math and language arts) who are

◆ patient, flexible, and positive
◆ entrepreneurial in spirit (since the evolution of a SSC mimics the development of a business in many ways)
◆ excellent collaborators
◆ focused on student outcomes
◆ responsive to data
◆ aware of school curriculum and practices
◆ willing to pour energy into a dynamic and difficult enterprise sure to improve learning outcomes for struggling learners.

Other schools that are implementing a SSC have attempted other approaches to staffing, though with mixed results. Some schools have various teachers work in the school library to help students during a plan period (for extra-duty pay), or have a special education teacher run a resource room for strug-gling students, or have an education assistant (not a full-time teacher) support struggling students. Each of these models certainly has merit and addresses the difficulty of allocating resources to a robust SSC. However, each lacks the necessary punch to make this intervention transformative. In our school, the SSC (though it involved a start-up cost and is not a cheap resource) is highly valued by parents, staff, students, and the community at large and has become a centerpiece of our RtI process. Once other high schools implement this structure with fidelity, they will never want to give it up.

The built-in flexibility of this system applies to staffing needs as well. As the math teacher in our center, I work with a wide variety of students because we have an open door policy (meaning any student can come see us for help during the day, as long as they have an open period or a study hall). I also carve out time to work with data sets in order to continually analyze and share information about our interventions and Tier 1 outcomes with the RtI leadership team, PLCs, department chairs, and building leaders. Data analy-sis (with decision-making and advising) has essentially become my plan period. Most schools in our district cannot afford to have an RtI coordinator who implements RtI all day without working with students. Instead, we have found a way to have a math teacher work with struggling students through-out the school day and also work on RtI implementation policies and data analysis. I have the freedom to choose when to pull students to remediate math skills. Therefore I can choose to allocate my time according to demands that range from student interventions all the way to systemic RtI implemen-tation issues. A classroom teacher does not have this degree of flexibility. Our language arts teacher also takes advantage of the flexibility within the SSC to occasionally offer literacy support in classrooms, sharing her expertise on differentiation and individualized instruction with other teachers and departments.

Some Key Requirements for the SSC

An effective student support center requires many components, all of which contribute to its impact on student achievement:

- Access to students through study hall or guided study hall
- Access to curriculum electronically or otherwise
- Access to progress-monitoring data and ability to respond with remediation tools
- Ongoing, intensive training of peer coaches
- Meaningful, targeted involvement of core teachers
- Viable connections with key stakeholders, such as counselors, administrators, PLCs, PST, and parents, as this is a shared building resource
- Open, welcoming environment for students that promotes indepen-dent learning habits
- Goal-oriented environment that encourages students to set goals and reach them
- Measurable outcomes
- Demographics and other tracking measures (who is using the SSC and how often?)

The Physical Environment of the SSC

The physical layout of your SSC will depend, of course, upon your own building layout, resources, and staffing. I will illustrate what works for our Student Support Center; you may want to consider how to integrate the fol-lowing plans with your own layout ideas.

> ### *Lessons Learned*
>
> For student support centers and other flexible intervention systems to be successful, make sure there is an adequate access point (like a study hall). This study hall should be run by an attentive staff member to increase accountability for students (they cannot be allowed to work the system to avoid support).

- A quiet, friendly, nonthreatening environment where students feel comfortable and safe in asking for help in a small-group or individual setting
- Separation between language arts and math areas. We split the room with partitions so as not to create two different rooms but to offer some amount of separation.
- Sign-in location near entrance
- Worktables for small-group work on both sides of the partition
- Movable or permanent white board for group math instruction as needed
- Computer workstations with intervention software; credit recovery software, if desired; and access to word processing, research, grade checking, and curriculum if on teacher web pages
- Bookkeeping area for peer coaches with a pass writing station and communication wall
- Data processing station with a filing system to organize class periods and student data
- Location to store basic supplies, including paper, pencils, dictionaries, graphing calculators, rulers, textbooks for all content areas for use by students and peer coaches, teachers' editions, and other learning and reference materials
- A warm and welcoming atmosphere with student art prominently displayed and a Celebration Wall highlighting student success

Accessing Students

Schools that attempt to build a student support center without having students scheduled into some type of study hall, guided study hall, access period, homeroom, or enrichment period, will struggle to reach the students most in need. It is crucial to develop a system for pulling students through established protocols with access points (study halls). Originally, we scheduled most freshmen into a study hall, giving them a full seven-period day and a spot where we could access struggling students. Since then we have expanded our targeted audience to tenth-grade students as well, and we are moving toward making study hall a mandatory placement based on risk factors and testing.

Developing a Mission Statement and Promoting the SSC

Developing a mission statement for the SSC is not meant to be a corporate directive, but rather a way to organize, clarify, and focus attention on the established goals of the center while aligning with the school's mission statement. You may want to consider splitting the mission statement into two areas, one for staff (and other stakeholders) and one for students. Once agreed upon, create and display large posters to advertise the SSC prominently throughout the school and in the center itself. Also, generate a pamphlet with the mission statement for parents and other stakeholders to promote the student support center as an accessible, dynamic means of helping students. The sample we created at the outset of our endeavor can be found as Figure 8.3. The mission statement's goals and measurements should then serve as the foundation for the rubric by which you evaluate your student support center's effectiveness.

From the start it is important to actively promote the student support center's services. Begin as early as possible and continue the promotion throughout the year using a variety of media. In other words, get the message out:

- ◆ Meet with departments to discuss the various roles of the SSC.
- ◆ Plan a larger group presentation to explain the purposes of the SSC as it relates to RtI. The mission statement is helpful for promotion but more details will likely be desired by the school staff. Such presentations should always include data and time to reflect on the need for a robust intervention system.
- ◆ Include regular announcements on the public address system to keep students and staff informed of the services provided by the SSC.
- ◆ Promote the center actively during open houses and parent–teacher conferences.
- ◆ Have a link on your school's website that details the mission statement and enables you to share data.
- ◆ Conduct early orientation for all freshmen in the study hall and for all new teachers in the school. This provides an overview of the SSC and highlights the resources available.

FIGURE 8.3. SSC Mission Statement

Palmer High School Student Support Center Mission Statement

For the Staff
We will create a friendly, helpful environment designed to foster student success. Through quality supplemental assistance based on classroom data and progress monitoring, the student support center will help to increase student achievement.

Target Goals and Measurement
   ◆ Build relationships with students
   ◆ Communicate with stakeholders
   ◆ Provide resources for teachers for interventions (staff RtI library)
   ◆ Evaluate integrity and fidelity of interventions in student support center
   ◆ Provide ongoing training and evaluation of peer coaches
   ◆ Coordinate with PLC groups (math and English to start, expanding later to more departments)
   ◆ Coordinate with special education, regular education, ESL, and GT programs to offer a continuum of intervention strategies
   ◆ Monitor progress (celebrate success, remediate deficiencies)
   ◆ Gather data on efficacy of student support center (How will we measure our success?)
      • Successmaker or other software programs
      • D/F reports
      • Dropout rates (credits earned at each grade level)
      • Achievement gap analysis (ethnic or socioeconomic achievement discrepancy)
      • Short-cycle curriculum-based measures (CBM)
      • Quantity and demographics of usage (number of students served at SSC)
      • Surveys, pros and cons from all stakeholders
      • CSAP score analysis
      • MAP data
   ◆ Respond to data and continuously improve service delivery

For the Students
The student support center is here to help you reach your goals, to encourage your independent learning, and to build confidence by offering the specific help you need when you need it. We are here as your advocates and to support your efforts.

Training of Peer Coaches

From the outset we wanted upperclassmen with impressive academic backgrounds to help deliver tutoring to struggling younger students as part of the SSC model. Compelling research backs the notion of structured peer tutoring (Gerber & Kauffman, 1981; Fuchs, Fuchs, & Burish, 2000; Hall & Stegila, 2003), but it requires considerable training and continual feedback to be successful. We have worked very closely with our counseling department to

> ### *Lessons Learned*
>
> When working with students as peer tutors, develop training tools and evaluation rubrics (keep the end in mind) to ensure fidelity.

recruit a capable group of student tutors whom we refer to as "peer coaches." These students, usually two or three juniors or seniors per period, help us write and run passes to collect the students and then become a cadre of effective tutors for a variety of subjects. Though we actively recruit students with strong academic backgrounds, we have also had success with those who have had to overcome serious obstacles to becoming upperclassmen. The keys to successful peer coaching are the following:

1. Proper training (initially and ongoing)
2. Feedback through rubrics and follow-through
3. Stressing the importance of confidentiality.

The SSC leaders should develop a set of training protocols to ensure that the training for peer coaches is effective and thorough. Student tutors have the potential to be an extremely valuable asset for the SSC and the school in general. The training guide is available at www.eyeoneducation.com.

Our training program asks student tutors to follow these guidelines:

- ◆ Provide specific, positive feedback to encourage and guide student learning.
- ◆ Never give students answers; you are a guide along the process.
- ◆ Never write on a student's paper; students must own the end product as well as the process.
- ◆ Feature various modalities: have students say it, see it, hear it, write it, touch it, and they will be more likely to remember it.
- ◆ Allow proper think time before expecting students to give responses.
- ◆ Scaffold: give only as much as students need to reach understanding.
- ◆ Fade away support once mastery is in sight; allow students the opportunity to become independent learners.
- ◆ Be positive, patient, and kind as you help struggling students; they have had very little experience with success and we are trying to help them build confidence and competence.
- ◆ Build relationships with the student; students often prefer working with a peer rather than a teacher.

Regarding feedback training, we ask the tutors to do a written reflection on two questions with time to discuss them afterward. This process is documented in peer coach folders.

a. Describe a time in which you received negative feedback from a teacher and discuss the impact it had on you.
b. Describe a time when you received meaningful, positive feedback from a teacher and discuss the impact it had on you.

The follow-up process involves many different role-playing scenarios that specifically address feedback and also other components of tutoring. While doing role-plays with peer coaches, I will usually start by acting the part of the struggling student and have a coach attempt to tutor me while other coaches record observations. We then offer positive feedback and chances for improvement. Then we reverse the roles and I play the role of a coach (intentionally making mistakes in the process of tutoring). Through this process, the coaches become aware of good and poor tutoring practices. I then ease them into the process of working with students using materials we have reviewed. The review of materials, specifically for math, involves PLC-agreed-upon methods for instructing various problem-solving techniques. We emphasize the importance of supporting the work of classroom instruction, though we certainly value alternate strategies if they aid student learning and honor differences in learning style.

We tend to partner the coaches with a variety of student groups, based on the coach's strengths and student needs. For instance, they are often effective with English language learners (ELLs), and are trained on the importance of reinforcing language during the math tutoring. They are often helpful with mid-level struggling students—those who are missing some key concepts but do not have a learning disability or significant learning struggle. I focus most of my personal tutoring energy on the latter group because they often require more intensive supports.

On the language arts side, peer coaches are excellent resources to help students with

◆ Research
◆ Editing and proofreading
◆ Vocabulary note cards and practice
◆ Guided reading assistance
◆ One-on-one motivation and organization talks
◆ Summarizing and note-taking strategies

The language arts teacher in the SSC spends time working individually with students who have deeper literacy deficits and are not receiving other Tier 2 literacy support (due to a lack of space to accommodate all students that need support). Chapters 9 and 10 will cover more of the specifics of how math and literacy supports work in the SSC.

Evaluation of Peer Coaches

To make time for peer coach evaluations, we build in time by doing a "no-pull" day in which we do not pull students from study hall. Through the use of the Peer Coach Evaluation Rubric (see www.eyeoneducation.com), we ask coaches to evaluate themselves and we then provide specific feedback. We also solicit ideas from the coaches to improve the student support center during this evaluation process. I recommend doing this evaluation at least twice per semester and having an open door policy regarding suggestions for improvement. Along the way, I also demonstrate each new math concept by going over homework and practice tests that freshmen and sophomore students are likely to need help with in the student support center. In order to make sure the students are improving as tutors, we conduct many observations, using the rubric to provide feedback and guide development. Along the way, it will become apparent that some of the peer coaches are not going to be effective working with struggling students. For them, I often assign more administrative and record-keeping duties, including running errands, grading CBMs, and data entry. In other words, there is a way to maximize productivity even if it is not explicitly through tutoring students.

The more time and energy you invest into training and evaluating peer coaches, the more effectively the Student Support Center functions. The students who need help are often more willing to work with a peer than with an adult. We have witnessed impressive growth in coaches as they take pride in helping younger, struggling students experience success. The coaches themselves tend to improve in all subject areas and also increase their own communication and interpersonal skills. Many of our peer tutors have expressed interest in becoming teachers because of their experience in the SSC. We now even occasionally "outsource" the coaches, once fully trained, to work with teachers in classrooms that have a significant number of struggling learners. This resource continues to evolve and prove itself of significant value to our success as a support system.

Collaboration

Our success in the student support center demands that we actively collaborate with a wide variety of stakeholders. To make a relevant and immediate difference for students, the SSC must be actively connected to curriculum. Here is a list of key stakeholders with whom we collaborate frequently:

- Obviously, we must build a great working relationship with at-risk students.
- We work closely with professional learning communities (PLCs) across a variety of contents and grade levels. By meeting with PLCs, we keep a close pulse-check on what students are expected to know and be able to do in order to be successful. This collaboration allows PLCs to suggest how the student support center can best help struggling students in particular content areas and vice versa.
- Often we will collaborate with individual teachers to improve interventions and focus on particular students.
- We work closely with the problem-solving team by providing insight into students' strengths and weaknesses and implementing interventions.
- We collaborate with the English as a Second Language (ESL) and Special Education Departments to flexibly support both groups of students.
- We work closely with deans and the at-risk coordinator to track down truant students and get them back on track.

Use of Teachers' Duty Hours in the SSC

In our school district, high school teachers are required, by contract, to provide non-classroom duty or supervision time. Traditionally, in our local high schools, this resource was underutilized on study hall supervision or hall duty. We have worked to maximize this resource by having core content–level teachers complete the duty hours in the student support center. Math, science, social studies, and English teachers spend one of their plan periods tutoring in the SSC in their specific content area. Utilizing staff duty hours in the student support center has provided multiple benefits (some of which are stated in Figure 8.2):

- Specialized support by highly qualified teachers paired with struggling students in need of intervention support
- More communication between the student support center and the Tier 1 teachers
- More communication between teachers across grade levels within each content area (vertical articulation), pushing many

dialogues forward regarding what we are teaching freshmen (how and why) and the rigor, accessibility, and relevance of the core curriculum
♦ More communication across content areas to push initiatives about problem-solving (math and science) and literacy strategies (English and social studies)
♦ More targeted use of the once neglected, yet valuable resource of teacher duty hours

The other teachers from elective (not core content) areas complete their duty hours as mentors to at-risk students or work with students in at-risk classroom settings and in the guided study halls. This required a separate scheduling system, run by an administrator, to tailor teacher strengths to student needs.

We met with each department separately at the beginning of the semester to construct a schedule and populate individual teachers into each SSC tutoring slot. These meetings allowed a chance to collaborate and provided teachers and departments a bit of choice as to which planning period and which semester to complete their duty hours. This resulted in a master schedule for teachers that covered each period of the day for each subject over the length of a semester (except for a few exceptions). Once we established the busiest periods of the day in the student support center (based on screening data), many teachers were flexible enough to meet the demands of struggling students by switching periods. We then provide an orientation session to familiarize teachers with the tutoring and support process.

Selecting and Monitoring Students in the SSC

Once the physical environment and basic organizational elements are in place, data analysis becomes the necessary next step. A considerable amount of time must be dedicated to data analysis at the outset to identify which students are likely to need support through the student support center and to determine access points for those students. This analysis also helps us anticipate the demand and workload required during each study hall period. We use spreadsheet software and queries through a database management system to compile the key information we have available for freshmen students (and sophomores if they are in a study hall). We look specifically for students who historically were not proficient on the state reading, writing, and math test (CSAP) and who were not already receiving intervention support elsewhere. It is highly advisable to train several staff members on programs such as Excel and Access to efficiently run queries and pivots (ideally, at least a few staff members in our building know these programs already) in order to do mass data analysis that will be used to make programming decisions for interventions.

A typical school year in the SSC goes through the following DBDM phases of identifying and working with students (ninth and tenth graders):

Phase 1

- ◆ Review freshman and sophomore databases for students without supports who are not proficient in math, reading, and writing (yet not in other intervention classes)
- ◆ Pull these students early and often to provide homework support, encourage better work ethic, and teach organization

Phase 2

- ◆ Respond to classroom test data and overall grades: which students fail to keep up with peers as measured by classroom grades (all the more relevant with a standards-based system)
- ◆ Begin to pull students who demonstrate weak skills on initial administration of progress-monitoring baseline measures (for reading, writing, and math); these data also allow us to fill in some gaps for students for whom we had no data initially
- ◆ Remediate those who lack prerequisite skills
- ◆ Track student progress on basic skills and pull students not progressing (since our CBM is administered every two weeks in math and our writing rubric monthly, we catch students new to our school with skill deficits on a fairly frequent basis)

Phase 3

- ◆ Monitor student grades to intervene with students falling behind in core content classes (again, we encounter new students in this cohort who were not previously identified)
- ◆ Assist students with work completion

Phase 4

 ◆ Review content prior to tests; teach test-taking strategies and study habits
 ◆ Re-teach students who have not met standards on assessments and retest them

These phases represent a cumulative pull because we continue the work of the early phases simultaneously as more phases are added. Furthermore, we also respond to referrals by teachers, counselors, administrators, parents, coaches, and students themselves (walk-ins). One trip to our SSC would illustrate the magical dynamic of witnessing so many students receiving support across a spectrum of tiers in a flexible, targeted manner.

Every two weeks I generate a new query of students based on extensive data, and this serves as my pull list for students (like a roster) from which the daily schedule is established. This is an organic document that I will continually populate (via spreadsheets and access databases) with

 ◆ grade information
 ◆ progress monitoring from math and language arts classes (for the other side of the student support center)
 ◆ additional benchmark data as they are added
 ◆ attendance information as the semester progresses.

Students are added to this list and others are only monitored periodically to ensure progress in the core curriculum. As students become more successful, we fade away the support and thus are able to concentrate more intensive energies upon students with persistent and pressing needs.

Evaluating effectiveness of the SSC

To collect student usage data, a method to input student visitors is needed. In our school, students scan their student identification cards when they enter the student support center and all the names are entered into a spreadsheet to help us track quantity, demographic, program, and ethnic information about usage. Having this information allows us to track grades, attendance, assessments, and credit requirements of students receiving services in the SSC. In other words, collecting data on student usage is one of the means to evaluate the effectiveness of the intervention. Because our SSC is open to all, including walk-in students who want a variety of help, we were somewhat surprised about the usage by program and grade area (especially considering we targeted struggling ninth graders without IEP or ELL labels).

DBDM For instance, of the ninth graders who visited the SSC during the first semester of operations, almost 34% were honors students (mostly self-selectors); the percentage of honors students was even higher for tenth and eleventh graders. International Baccalaureate (IB) is our most advanced educational program, and more than 20% of our tenth-grade visitors were IB students. The majority of these groups, honors and IB, were seeking math help. These figures illustrate the benefits of having a flexible, open door policy for a student support center.

As we expected, since the SSC began as a freshman-based, at-risk intervention program, we saw mostly freshmen. They were pulled from study halls to build study habits and work ethic, as well as to develop academic skills. For this reason, nearly 65% of all visitors to the student support center were freshmen in our first year. However, we were surprised that without really promoting the resource actively to the rest of the grade levels, we saw 35% of our students from upper grade levels (similar results have continued for each year of operation). Students seek help on their own on a regular basis above and beyond those we target. Tracking these types of demographic numbers provides useful data for making staffing and resource allocation decisions.

Quantitative Impact

All statistical reviews of data demonstrate that the student support center has been effective in helping struggling students, usually the most at-risk population in our building, to pass content classes. It has also helped at-risk students (and low-performing students) to make more growth on the state's standard assessment as compared to their peers. Additionally, students who frequented the SSC had the following achievements:

- ◆ Significant reduction in at-risk rating between entering ninth grade and exiting ninth grade
- ◆ Nearly all ability ranges of ninth-grade SSC visitors averaged enough credits to become sophomores (eleven credits needed)
- ◆ Sharp decline in number of students failing ninth and tenth grade (credit deficient)

◆ A marked increase in standardized assessment scores for groups we saw frequently for math and reading
◆ Significant growth in reading and math assessments as compared to peers across the state (Colorado longitudinal growth model)

The student support center alone does not define RtI in our school. It operates as part of a continuum of Tier 1 and Tier 2 interventions. A variety of interventions (math, literacy, and behavioral) offer a spectrum of services at differing degrees of intensity. What the SSCenter uniquely offers is a flexible structure to complement math and literacy interventions, while offering organization, motivation, grade tracking, and credit recovery options. The varied and tiered offerings for math and literacy support in our building (beyond the SSC) are extensive and probaby would constitute a book unto themselves. The following two chapters demonstrate in more detail how math and literacy interventions are complemented and enhanced through the student support center.

9

Tiered High School Math Interventions

The success of the student support center and math interventions in general largely depends on the collaboration of the math department. Driven by a PLC culture, tiered math interventions naturally support and enhance common, formative curriculum assessments, pacing, and standards-based grading. Furthermore, PLCs that integrate authentic problem-solving opportunities and research-based elements of math instruction across tiers improve opportunities for all students to learn. A summary of key research-based strategies for math instruction and interventions is available as Appendix C.

At first glance, placement of students into a continuum of math supports could be confused with tracking. However, for schools implementing RtI effectively, placement of students is not a life sentence. Math departments must consider how course programming and placement facilitate upward mobility for students. This includes the means to ensure

- ♦ Students who are behind peers catch up
- ♦ Students who are at grade level make at least one year's gain
- ♦ Student who are advanced are provided chances for enrichment

Flow charts and descriptions of courses help organize the placement guidelines, including expected outcomes and evaluation metrics. One such description follows as Figure 9.1 (this figure does not include special education, advanced, or honors offerings).

When placing students into a math continuum, we consider how to meet student needs and how to efficiently allocate resources. This demands a variety of Standard Protocol Treatment (STP) options as well as flexible support like the student support center (SSC). Throughout the years it has become clear that the most important aspect of any math intervention is the personality of the teacher. The department leadership recognizes this and, paying attention to personality and training, consistently places the most qualified teachers with the students with the greatest needs, a model reversed in typical high school math departments.

A brief description of our ever-evolving continuum follows in order of degree of intensity, with a focus upon the general education population.

Placement into a Continuum of Math Offerings

The creation of a cohesive mathematics program demands a diverse continuum of class offerings in addition to a flexible intervention system. For entering freshmen in our school, there are six options for placement, depending on a student's ability and desire. Top students with significant motivation can select an International Baccalaureate (IB) high-level math class. There are also two different honors offerings. The majority of incoming freshmen (65%) are enrolled in the integrated algebra geometry course. Those with more significant needs and struggles are placed into a sheltered pre-algebra course (Mastery Algebra) or a sheltered version of pre-algebra for special education students or one for English language learners (ELL). Figure 9.1 on page 133 shows our continuum of math services for entering freshmen.

This type of framework can greatly assist with resource allocation and prioritization. It was developed collaboratively by the math department, intervention teachers, and the SSC. It forced us to be more specific and targeted about how and why we place students, what the intervention really looks like, and what results are to be measured. For the purposes of brevity, this chapter will not discuss the honors, ELL, or special education placement in detail. The focus will be upon those "unlabeled" students who are as such unsupported.

Tier 1: PLCs and Strategies in the Classroom

All of our algebra teachers are not necessarily teaching the exact same thing every day in the exact same way. However, they all use common language and common teaching approaches and work from an agreed-upon set of essential understandings. The Big Ideas are approved from the outset of a unit with an eye toward the standards. The assessment is developed based on those standards and Big Ideas. The PLC then fosters rigorous discussion about pedagogy and best practices for lessons and how to ensure understanding rather than just memorization. The goal is to arrive at agreement on the best instructional method for a given strategy (based on research, data, and

FIGURE 9.1. Math Interventions by Tiers

	Tier 1	Tier 2	Tier 3
Offering	McREL strategies and research-based math strategy instruction	Mastery Algebra (double block) Math Tutorial Student Support Center	Modified algebra class Software program such as ALEKS or Successmaker Student support center
Responsible Party	Classroom teachers for all content areas	Math interventionist SSC teacher	Special education and SSC math teacher
Groupings	Whole class	Small group (15–20) Between 3 and 5 for SSC support (identified through screening data)	Small group and one-on-one (identified through screening and progress-monitoring data)
Frequency	Embedded in classroom instruction on a regular basis	Mastery Algebra: daily for 100 minutes Math Tutorial: daily for 50 minutes SSC: twice per week for 30 minutes	Daily, same as Tier 2, except SSC support increased to one-on-one support daily
Assessment	Universal screen such as Measure of Academic Progress by NWEA Twice per year Curriculum-based measures of progress of pre-algebra skills every month to measure response to instruction Use of standards-based assessment to monitor progress	In addition to Tier 1 assessments: Metrics from progress-monitoring CBMs and from standards-based monitoring	In addition to Tier 1 assessments, metrics from math software administered weekly to measure response to intervention Could include AIMSweb or others
Expected Outcomes	At least one year's growth on math measures, as determined by state tests or NWEA MAP	More than one year's growth and gains on MAP	More than one year's growth and gains on MAP

professional judgment) and to teach it with fidelity. Taking into account the Big Ideas, common vocabulary, standards, assessments, and teaching, materials are then created or edited from textbooks and Internet sources, resulting in a collaborative planning effort among teachers.

The guiding principle among the math PLCs is to teach for understanding and evaluate student performance according to standards. Teachers grade in a nonpunitive manner and they extend the opportunity for students to demonstrate mastery of the Big Ideas throughout an entire semester. This method makes for more difficult grading but serves to inform students, parents, administrators, and interventionists about the specific degree of understanding of each student. The tiered support system we offer provides a wide range of opportunities for students to increase mastery of algebra and pre-algebraic concepts. Students who fail in this type of freshman algebra program usually do so because of a complete lack of effort or extensive attendance problems.

The Flexible Approach: Student Support Center (Tier 1, 2, and occasionally 3)

For all other students not enrolled in the previously mentioned interventions who failed to reach the proficiency standard on the state test (often close to 25% of the freshman algebra population), we provide a flexible level of support in the student support center. The SSC is our most dynamic offering because we pull students from study hall in order to offer preventive support and remediation so they can succeed in the regular algebra class. This support is also provided to any student who begins to struggle in the class for any reason. We work hard to identify students who might potentially struggle in order to intervene early and often with pre-algebraic skills that are monitored via our progress-monitoring tools (administered in the algebra class). However, many students struggle due to illness, family issues, or just maturity struggles (though they score well on state and national math tests). We also help these students get on their feet, though the support looks different and may be less frequent. The dynamic nature of the intervention has allowed us to reach more students (and in more math classes) and has significantly reduced the freshman failure rates.

Next Line of Support: Math Tutorial (Tier 2)

Students just above this level, those scoring partially proficient (low) on the state assessment, are placed in the regular algebra class with the support of the Math Tutorial class. The Math Tutorial, as mentioned in previous chapters, provides just-in-time remediation of pre-algebraic skills aligned with the course. Coupled with the remediation, the intervention class also offers guided homework support and test preparation. The teacher works closely with students in small groups for differentiated remediation and also conducts whole-class instruction based on areas of need. This intervention acts as a supplemental support and utilizes progress-monitoring data to ensure effective implementation. Students track their own data and the teacher differentiates instruction based on an item analysis of the data from the progress-monitoring tools (more on this later in the chapter).

For Students Two Years Behind: Mastery Math (Tier 2 and Tier 3)

Students who do not have a disability and are not ELL but who score in the "unsatisfactory" range on our state math test (often representing a two-year lag) as eighth graders are enrolled in the double block Mastery Algebra course for the freshman year. This offering is a double dose of pre-algebra remediation with an ultimate goal of shrinking the gap and helping students catch up with their peers by the end of the freshman year. In years past we offered a modified course for these students that focused on core freshman curriculum without promoting true remediation. Though there were merits to this model (and it produced some degree of success), on the whole the data suggested that more robust remediation was needed to help these students catch up. By adjusting the bar (without a double block of remediation), we never really addressed the problem but rather passed it on to higher grade levels. The Mastery Algebra course has allowed us to meet students where they are mathematically while at the same time accelerating the remediation so they are better prepared for more robust algebra demands for the rest of their high school careers. The course demands that students reach a minimal proficiency (80–90%) on a variety of essential pre-algebraic skills in order to pass the class. They are given limitless opportunities during the semester to demonstrate mastery and are provided small-group remediation to help them reach mastery. Progress monitoring is implemented throughout the course as well as student tracking of learning (more on this later in the chapter).

For Students Who Struggle the Most: Core Algebra with Remediation

For students entering high school more than two or three years behind their peers, we follow a course which focuses on two goals:

1. Meet students where they are with remedial and responsive software (such as ALEKS) to patch gaps in basic mathematics in a differentiated manner.
2. Teach a reduced number of core algebra concepts (power standards) at a modified pace with spiraled review (depth over breadth) in an engaging and project-based manner and with explicit instruction of problem solving strategies.

This lab (software) component represents 50-60% of the course, and the core algebra instruction fills the remaining time. Teachers respond flexibly to data as they work with students in stations during remediation days while also pressing for high levels of core algebra understanding. Students are less frustrated trying to understand material far above their comprehension while gaining exposure to key algebraic concepts. Although students are encouraged to do remediation outside of class (ALEKS is web-based), this course is offered as a single block of mathematics because many of the students lack room in their schedules for additional remediation due to IEPs, behavior, and reading interventions. In general, the students we place into the course:

- ◆ Have an IEP with a significant math concern
- ◆ Have fallen further behind each year, even after many different interventions
- ◆ Join late in a semester and have significant gaps in math due to transience or other issues
- ◆ Have experienced lack of access to public education for a variety of reasons (refugee status, homelessness, etc.)

This course best meets the needs of students who come to us every day with two backpacks; one we can see and one we cannot.

Evolution of Math Services Provided through the Student Support Center

The SSC has slowly shifted the type of math support provided to students. The evolutionary process has been focused on improvement since its inception. To accomplish our goals requires a close working relationship with the math department. The teachers in the department, recognizing the SSC as a powerful resource, willingly collaborate in order to maximize the resource's potential. The fruit of this labor is an enhanced approach to monitoring progress and a standards-based grading system that measures learning, growth, and understanding better than traditional grading and intervention models. The math experience in the SSC can be broken down into three distinct phases over two years.

Phase 1: Curriculum support

Goal: Improve student performance in the freshman algebra classroom
Measure of success: Grades (increase the percent of students passing algebra)
- Homework support
- Pretest
- Re-teach and retest
- Some use of computer tutoring software for remediation of skills (extra credit provided in the grade book)

Phase 2: Remediation

Goal: Remediate deficient pre-algebra skills
Measure of success: Growth on CBM (see Appendix B) and class grades
- Actionable data from day one that opens the door for remediation
- Remediate and monitor pre-algebra skills, which are also embedded in Tier 1 instruction
- Students track progress
- Rapidly respond to those not making progress

Phase 3: Standards-Based

Goal: Improve student performance on standards-based elements
Measure of success: Class grades, benchmark assessments (MAP), state math test (CSAP)
- Respond to specific areas (standards) of concern within curriculum (essentials)
- Focusing on strands of standards, re-teach and prepare for retest opportunity (delivered in the classroom via a formative assessment)
- Increase scope beyond ninth grade through the vehicle of standards-based interventions
- Run ACT math study sessions the entire month leading up to ACT exams (a Colorado requirement for juniors). Use computer modules, ACT prep materials, and small-group tutoring. All work done in the SSC should be connected to classroom grades.

◆ Actively pull sophomores during their open period in order to provide support prior to exams and afterward for re-teaching of missed concepts

◆ Remediation based on standards for all courses that are aligned to standards (grade 9–11 Integrated Algebra and Geometry offerings)

Just because we have entered Phase 3 does not mean we have ceased the other two phases. On the contrary, we layer each of these phases of support in a flexible way to meet the needs of a wide variety of students. In other words, though we have begun work on standards-based remediation, we still assist students with homework and remediation, and we will remain open to all students who seek any type of help. Beyond a close-working partnership with the math department, what this demands of the person responsible for running the SSC math portion is efficiency and organization. Streamlining this intense, flexible, and diverse intervention program is the central task of the SSC math teacher.

Throughout the first phase, we recognized that we needed to be doing more to improve the intervention delivery. It was effective at helping students with the content, but there was not much room for remediation. Thus we placed more focus on pre-algebra skill development during the second phase. The reason we were able to deepen the remediation was because of the progress-monitoring tools. They served as a vehicle for communication with the math teachers and the SSC as an intervention. Before the widespread use of the CBM instrument (see Appendix B), our remediation efforts were not explicitly tied to classroom curriculum and grades. Throughout this second phase, we also recognized that there was room to grow. While working with students on content and some skill remediation, we noticed that the focus was merely upon classroom grades. To shift this conversation, the SSC worked in conjunction with the math department to develop a standards-based approach to grading and intervening. This phase is pushing us to offer a more effective menu of options to struggling students. It demands more organization and flexibility because students have multiple chances to attain proficiency on all the standards.

We have gotten more aggressive about data collection and analysis, and this approach helps to inform our action plan for the freshman math PLC. We are able to serve students through various interventions with varying degrees of intensity. That is the beauty of our system. We can reach out to more students, before they need the help and/or as they need the help, and then fade away the support to encourage more independent learning habits. The SSC, paired with an effective PLC structure and standards-based grading, is an ideal mechanism to efficiently support all students.

10

Tiered High School Literacy Interventions

This chapter will not look to provide a comprehensive review of literacy support at the high school level. Rather, this will be a snapshot of how the student support center can best complement and enhance an existing tiered framework of literacy interventions.

Generally speaking, high schools are not typically poised to remediate literacy deficits. The core components of reading (phonemic awareness, phonics, fluency, vocabulary, and comprehension) may be well known to primary school teachers, but high schools are often departmentalized and content-specific. Several researchers, in fact, point to these limitations as evidence that RtI is limited in its ability to offer a comprehensive array of literacy services for high school (O'Brien, Stewart, & Moje, 1995). Literacy does not necessarily have a home department like mathematics. Thus literacy is often an unclaimed field relegated to special educators and adolescent reading interventionists, especially regarding the first three components mentioned above. There is also very little research to suggest RtI is an effective literacy intervention system for high school students (Cobb, Sample, Alwell, & Johns, 2005). So why would schools that must provide "research-based" literacy practices experiment with RtI? From our experience, the answer is clear: because RtI has the potential to streamline resources and evaluate their effectiveness.

Delivering effective literacy interventions at the high school level is considerably more difficult than delivering math interventions for a variety of reasons. The fact that literacy is not really "owned" by one particular department means that the accountability is not centralized (unlike in mathematics). When the standardized test scores roll in for reading and writing, who is accountable? the English, social studies, science, math, or other departments?

Of course the answer usually comes back, "we all are responsible for literacy". Unfortunately, this is another way to say that no one is responsible for literacy. Furthermore, schools must flexibly deliver a range of literacy services, and this is not typically a strength for high schools. It certainly was a struggle in our school before the creation of the student support center.

One way to increase ownership of literacy is to institute schoolwide literacy programs such as the strategic instruction model (SIM) created by the Kansas University Center for Research on Learning. As a research-validated model to increase adolescent literacy, SIM makes content-area literacy instruction explicit and a leading priority for all teachers. Rather than brushing aside reading concerns, schools that employ SIM bring attention to the need for explicit strategy instruction regarding comprehension and improving content delivery. Under the term "routines," SIM implores teachers of content to teach understanding, recall, and organization in a learner-friendly manner. In other words, SIM helps to ensure that literacy is a schoolwide priority.

Leaders in the field of adolescent literacy (Lenz, Ehren, & Deschler, 2005; Deshler & Hughes, 2007) have proposed the use of a content literacy continuum to further improve structure for tiered literacy supports for the high school setting. It involves five key stages:

1. Enhanced content instruction
2. Embedded strategy instruction
3. Intensive tutoring in strategies
4. Basic skills instruction
5. Therapeutic intervention (speech and language pathologist)

This model suggests RtI is possible at the high school level for literacy. Other researchers suggest that the very nature of high schools makes the first two components (phonemic awareness and phonics) especially difficult, and thus literacy support is de facto just a Tier 2 support system (Brozo, 2010) rather than a rich, tiered system of instruction and intervention. Brozo goes on to caution against the RtI model for high school literacy because of its simplistic emphasis on basic, elementary skills. He believes, as do other researchers (Gee, 2001; McCarthey & Moje, 2002), that adolescent literacy is much more complex and demanding of flexible, creative offerings that seek to authentically connect readers to text. In fact, Brozo also points to the fallibility in believing that only scientifically based (another core tenet of RtI) reading strategies will increase adolescent reading achievement.

Given these concerns, for tiered literacy support to succeed in high schools with fidelity, it demands the following:

1. Robust content instruction embedded with literacy strategies school-wide (Tier 1)
2. A flexible approach to literacy support that works to motivate, inspire, and engage students as well as teach scientifically based core strategies more intensely (Tier 2)
3. A reliable standard treatment protocol for reading skills that meets students where they are and authentically links scientifically based remediation in core reading areas with core content knowledge acquisition. (Tier 3)

Evolution of RtI-Based Literacy in Our High School

On top of schoolwide literacy instruction across contents in our high school, our English department is responsible for teaching a reading program called Read 180 and our special education department offers lower remediation-based reading classes (programs like Reading Navigator). So we offer strategic programmatic support to students who are two or more grade levels behind as well as the content literacy support offered at Tier 1. However, we have limited resources and thus are unable to provide all the slots required to support struggling students, and convincing all core content teachers to jump on board with literacy strategies is no small task.

Furthermore, because of stigma, many high school–age teenagers do not want the services of a full reading intervention. Thus the students that we are unable to reach via the traditional standard treatment protocol for reading supports struggle mightily in the core content classes. The rigorous demands of comprehension, vocabulary development, inference, and extended writing become overwhelming. Because this particular type of student is likely to drop out, we needed to develop a more targeted and flexible literacy intervention system.

Early in our RtI process, the data demonstrated a gap between how many slots we were able to offer and how many students needed support. As mentioned in Chapter 8, the student support center was developed to meet the needs of more students in a flexible manner. As a literacy support structure, it has evolved over the past three years to become more targeted and efficient, with great potential to offer even greater supports to struggling students.

Teachers across departments recognize the SSC as a powerful resource and collaborate in order to maximize its potential. Though the process of building a high functioning relationship with the SSC has been slower for

English, Social Studies and Science, the changes have been deep and important. Each department now has implemented effective means of progress monitoring one particular literacy skill that can be addressed at Tier 1 and through the SSC. Our experience in the SSC can be broken down into two distinct phases spread over three years. The advances in the SSC approach to literacy support have demanded a parallel evolution of instruction and curriculum from three departments—English, social studies, and science.

Collaboration itself has become more challenging because of the sheer volume of connections. More teachers and more curricula make it difficult to effectively help all students in the three subject areas. However, in the SSC we noticed that students who struggled with basic organization, motivation, work ethic, and literacy tended to need help in all subjects all year long. What has been instrumental across all three phases of literacy evolution is the explicit link to student motivation, interest, and engagement.

Phase 1: Curriculum Support

Goal: Improve student performance in English, social studies, and science
Measure of success: Grades (increase success rates)
   ◆ Homework support
   ◆ Research assistance for projects
   ◆ Guided reading assistance
   ◆ Vocabulary review
   ◆ Test preparation, strategy instruction

Phase 2: Standards-based

Goal: Improve student performance on standards-based reading and writing elements
Measure of success: Class grades, benchmark assessments (MAPs), state reading and writing tests (CSAP)
   ◆ Respond to curriculum-based measures of reading comprehension (such as CLOZE) and rubric-analyzed writing samples to improve basic literacy components
   ◆ Respond to specific areas (standards) of concern within curriculum (essentials)
   ◆ Increase scope beyond ninth grade through the vehicle of standards-based interventions
   ◆ Increase the targeted instruction of vocabulary acquisition

Phase 3: Strategies (across disciplines)

Goal: Improve student transfer of comprehension and vocabulary strategies into classroom setting
Measure of success: Class grades, benchmark assessments (MAPs), state reading and writing tests (CSAP)

As is true with math support, these three phases are not mutually exclusive. Supporting students with homework and work ethic is still in place when the more standardized remediation is implemented.

The SSC literacy teacher supports the contents of English, social studies, and science. This support often takes the shape of work completion and reading comprehension strategy instruction. However, the ultimate benefit of the SSC model is that it offers extreme flexibility. If your particular school has an affinity for a specific strategy or program, it can be supported by a student center.

In some cases, the SSC utilizes peer coaches to model guided reading approaches and study skills. This help is in addition to software support such as Successmaker for additional reading remediation. These efforts are especially beneficial for English language learners and students with disabilities. Though both groups receive significant support within our building, many are fully included in the general curriculum and benefit from the flexibility offered by the SSC.

Reading Comprehension and Vocabulary Acquisition

Whatever assessments are in place in your high school should guide the progress monitoring of literacy components. In high schools, it is not realistic to monitor all five elements of reading for all students, nor is it desirable. Again, consider the medical model: healthy patients do not need monthly checkups. However, for sick patients we need evidence that the treatment is working—thus more frequent checkups. Indeed, this is our greatest challenge to date: how to monitor reading for high school students and intervene accordingly. Some options are in place for special education students (MAZE and CLOZE probes), and other suggestions include randomly monitoring a student's acquisition of a semester's worth of vocabulary randomly every month, and every two weeks for those in need of additional support.

Though slower than in our mathematics department, the use of standards across other content areas has taken root in our school. The use of

FIGURE 10.1. Tiered Literacy Support

	Tier 1	Tier 2	Tier 3
Offering	McREL literacy strategies Strategic Instruction Model (SIM) as schoolwide literacy Content literacy continuum	Standard treatment protocol such as Read 180 Student support center provides additional support with written expression, reading comprehension, and vocabulary acquisition (part of content literacy continuum)	Targeted reading programs for phonics and fluency (e.g., Reading Navigator or Language!) Other software-based literacy program such as Successmaker Special education services (speech language)
Responsible Party	Classroom teachers for all content areas	Reading Interventionist (or English department) SSC literacy teacher	Special education
Groupings	Whole class	Small group (less than 20 for Read 180) Between 3 and 5 for SSC support	Small group and one-on-one
Frequency	Embedded in classroom instruction on a regular basis	Read 180: daily for 90 minutes SSC: twice per week for 30 minutes	Daily, time spent depends on specific program
Assessment	Universal screen such as MAP by NWEA Twice per year Curriculum-based measures of progress in reading and writing at least three times per semester to measure response to instruction	In addition to Tier 1 assessments, Metrics from reading program administered twice per month to measure response to intervention Vocabulary probes	In addition to Tier 1 assessments, metrics from reading program administered weekly to measure response to intervention Could include MAZE or CLOZE probes
Expected Outcomes	At least one year's growth on reading and writing measures, as determined by state tests or NWEA MAPs	More than one year's growth and gains on the SRI as well as MAPs	More than one year's growth and gains on the SRI as well as MAPs

standards-based grading and assessment in each content area *as the progress monitoring tool* will eventually replace the fear of progress monitoring. All our attention will be upon how students are progressing toward proficiency and what to do if they are not (or if they are beyond proficiency already).

Figure 10.1 is a table of some potential tiered literacy options and associated responsibilities and expectations.

Placement of students into reading interventions should follow similar guidelines listed in Chapters 7 and 9. The overall structure of Figure 10.1 also follows Batsche's diagram (Figure 5.1) relating to the intensity of intervention and assessment necessary to meet the needs of struggling students. Hand schedule the most at-risk students first, fill all slots, and then determine how many students will need additional, flexible support. Cut scores and placement decisions are largely to be determined by each school or by a district-wide policy. Because assessments vary to such a great extent from state to state, a specific recipe for placing students into interventions would not be sensible in this book. However, as a practical approach, it is advisable to sort students by a literacy risk factor (based on a wide variety of assessments and classroom performance) and identify all students at risk of struggling with literacy in your building. Sort them by grade and by priority to make informed decisions about how to fill the limited slots available.

Conclusion

Ultimately, high schools will struggle most with implementing the RtI framework for literacy because it demands involvement from all departments. Also, the challenges of monitoring progress for reading and writing are authentic and significant in the high school setting. For the process to be practical and relevant for the classroom teacher, tools must be developed to address these concerns. RtI in literacy also offers a promising avenue of research.

The challenge notwithstanding, schools must design and implement a continuum of literacy support schoolwide, even if perfect means to measure effectiveness (a rigorous standards-based assessment framework) are lacking.

11

Sustainability, Conclusions and Future of High School RtI

Response to Intervention is a complex, challenging, lengthy process of high school restructuring. We have seen firsthand, however, how it can transform the focus of a building and increase accountability and efficiency. It integrates systems and drives continuous improvement through data-based decision-making. It brings teams of professionals together with families and community members to support student learning. It ensures that a school's resources are targeted and tiered in the most effective way to meet the needs of a wide variety of students. And it provides a framework for assessments that mimics a medical model, increasing intensity proportionally to the degree of a student's needs.

For students, RtI offers the promise of preventive support and high-quality instruction. It ensures that students are not unfairly labeled with a disability while providing tiered intervention support even for students who do not qualify for special education services. Though it is not yet a perfect means to determine if a student has a learning disability, there is considerable hope (and some empirical evidence at earlier grades) that it will improve upon the previous eligibility process.

RtI creates a uniform and evolving instructional program coherence that drives relevant and cohesive professional development for all educators. It aligns all the goals and systems of a building singularly upon the mission of increasing student achievement and progress. RtI demands much of high schools, but it has potential to return results such as (but not limited to) the following:

- ◆ Increased graduation rates
- ◆ Improved instruction, curriculum, and intervention delivery across all tiers
- ◆ More targeted, usable, relevant, and reliable assessments
- ◆ Continuous improvement (data-based decision-making)
- ◆ Reduced number of students incorrectly labeled with a learning disability

In some ways RtI sounds too good to be true, almost a panacea. The reality check comes from the fact that the benefits come at the cost of cultural change and diligent, frank discussions about data-driven improvement. Working to continuously improve is an exhausting enterprise. There is no place to hide; there are no sacred cows; RtI demands accountability at all levels and it requires strong leadership to bring this degree of accountability into settings that have traditionally been exempt. Though it may be true that planning, implementation, and sustainability rest with leadership, RtI is a significant undertaking that requires the support of the entire school community. Once RtI has been implemented and enters into the sustainability phase, its primary purpose becomes continuous improvement, professional development, and system evaluation. The RtI journey is thus never finished as it works to embed a culture of improvement across the entire school setting.

Though education never seems to move fast enough, there are many positive and encouraging changes occurring in our school. Our school continues to evolve its approach to RtI. Our PLCs are becoming more responsive with data, more standards based in regards to curriculum, and an increasing number of regular educators are becoming involved in the promotion of RtI. A diverse group of general educators might give a presentation to staff during professional development on incorporating differentiation; another teacher might offer a mini-lesson about how to effectively phase in standards-based grading practices. As these examples show, our school is meaningfully aligning its systems. Our administrators are building the infrastructure to increase accountability, streamline professional development, and incorporate more data to drive reforms. The problem-solving teams are becoming more focused and time-oriented, and they meaningfully involve more regular educators, parents, and students. Our special education department is recognizing a change in how most regular education teachers discuss struggling students: labeling is no longer the first thought in a teacher's mind. Our standard treatment protocol intervention classes utilize progress-monitoring tools to evaluate student success on a regular basis and make adjustments accordingly. Our student support center is also increasing its focus upon standards, strategies, and remediation to improve learning outcomes for struggling students as we expand the resource to reach students beyond ninth grade. In other words, RtI as a systemwide approach of continuous improvement is maturing in our building as fidelity is taking center stage. The transformation continues.

Indeed, the future of RtI is much brighter for high schools embarking on the journey today compared to those that dabbled with this reform five to ten years ago. Response to Intervention is naturally suited to dovetail into existing and emerging reform movements in grading and assessment practices and the rise of Professional Learning Communities. An ever-expanding accessible bank of proven teaching strategies continue to empower professional development opportunities. Data is readily available to educators and schools are increasingly invested in basing decisions upon data. Given the strengthening of these foundational elements, including improvements in progress monitoring tools and a growing belief in a tiered model of service delivery, schools are now poised to take on the challenge of RtI. Once advancements in grade book and education-oriented data base systems fully catch up to the rigorous needs of RtI implementation, schools will have the tools necessary to meaningfully experience the promise of RtI.

Appendix A

Criteria for the Determination of SLD

Adopted with revisions from SLD Guidelines/Colorado Department of Education (10/7/08)

1) The child does not achieve adequately for the child's age or to meet State-approved grade level standards in one or more of the following areas, when provided with learning experiences and instruction appropriate for the child's age or state-approved grade-level standards

AND

2) The child does not make sufficient progress to meet age or state-approved grade-level standards in the area(s) identified when using a process based on the child's response to scientific, research-based intervention. In one or more of the following areas:

Areas of SLD:

- ◆ Oral Expression
- ◆ Listening Comprehension
- ◆ Written Expression
- ◆ Basic Reading Skill
- ◆ Reading Fluency Skills
- ◆ Reading Comprehension
- ◆ Mathematical Calculation
- ◆ Mathematical Problem Solving

In accordance with the two criteria stated above, Colorado ECEA Rules require a body of evidence demonstrating academic skill deficit(s) and insufficient progress when using a process based on the child's response to scientific, research-based intervention in one or more areas of specific learning disabilities.

When considering the student results that rely on a student's response to scientific, research-based intervention, the multidisciplinary team needs to be able to ensure that:

(1) there was a research/evidence base for the interventions implemented; and

(2) the interventions were implemented with fidelity, i.e., implemented as intended or prescribed with attention to the what, how, and intensity of instruction.

Guidance in the Determination of an Academic Skill Deficit

One issue that makes it difficult to establish the existence of a Specific Learning Disability is its multi-dimensional nature. "Most of the research on SLDs, particularly those affecting reading, shows that they occur along a continuum of severity rather than presenting as an explicit dichotomous category delineated by clear cut-points on the achievement distribution." (Fletcher et al, p. 28).

Because of this lack of discrete cut-points, the decision as to what constitutes a "significant" deficit is a complex one and will require a degree of professional judgment. However, the decision needs to be based on valid and reliable data.

In identifying the existence of SLD, a determination must be made that a student continues to have a significant academic skill deficit even after obtaining evidence of effective instruction in the general education classroom and the provision of targeted and/or intensive intervention. Below are some parameters for deciding the significance of a deficit. These are NOT intended to be absolute cut-points and the convergence of multiple sources of data needs to be considered by the eligibility team.

At least one measure needs to reflect a comparison to state/national benchmarks or norms in order to provide some consistency across schools and districts in the interpretation of "significance."

◆ Curriculum-Based Measurement (CBM) results that include at least 6 data points that are at or below the 12th percentile (based on national norms) may be considered significant.

◆ Criterion Reference Measures (CRMs) compare a student's performance to the goals of the curriculum. These may be provided within program materials or set by teachers. A significant deficit would be indicated by results that are at or below 50% of the grade level expectancy. Thus, grade level criteria must be determined for CRMs. (For example, if the expectation is that a student answer grade level comprehension questions with 80% accuracy and a student's accuracy through repeated trials is at 40% or less, then a significant deficit might be indicated.)

◆ When a measure is utilized that provides a percentile rank, such as an individually administered norm referenced test, a score at or below the 12th percentile may be considered to represent a significant deficit.

Again, the finding of an academic skill deficit should not be based on any one measure.

Guidance in the Determination of Insufficient Progress

Problem-solving teams monitor student progress toward norms/benchmarks. Insufficient progress can be determined by identifying expected rates of progress and by utilizing a Gap Analysis. When implementing a Gap Analysis, three types of norms/benchmarks may be used: research-based norms, local norms, or criterion-referenced benchmarks.

◆ Research-based norms: Research is available that identifies average rates of student progress in basic academic skills over time. (However, these norms should be used with caution whenever they are based on small sample sizes.) Research-based norms can be a helpful starting point for estimating expected student rates of growth. Examples of this type of norm can be found on AIMSweb for reading, math, spelling, and written language.

◆ Local norms: Some districts may have developed local norms, which allow teams to use the grade-level norms for the district in determining the goal the student is working toward. Evaluation teams will be able to calculate a rate of weekly improvement the student must attain to close the gap with their peers and the expected target.

◆ Criterion-referenced benchmarks: Benchmarks that are set as a standard of mastery against which a student's performance on an academic task or behavior can be compared. The evaluation team sets weekly rates of student improvement necessary to achieve the benchmark in a reasonable time period. The time period would be determined based on the significance of the gap to begin with. [Disadvantage: The setting of benchmarks can be somewhat arbitrary. Advantage: They can be applied flexibly to a very wide range of student academic skills and behaviors for which formal peer norms are unavailable.]

Wright, Jim. *RTI Toolkit* (2007)

Gap Analysis

The following is an example of applying Gap Analysis in order to determine a student's response to an intervention, as well as determining what the intensity level of an intervention should be.

- ◆ The Gap Analysis is calculated by dividing the expected benchmark (preferably based on national norms) by the student's current performance. The following steps provide a structure for determining the Gap along with the method of determining realistic growth expectations.

EXAMPLE:

A student is in second grade and is reading 20 words per minute (wpm) based on an Oral Reading Fluency probe given during the winter screening.

1. Determine the degree to which this student's performance differs from that of peers. If 75–80% of peers are achieving benchmark, then this student's performance is significantly different. If, however, this student's performance reflects the same level as 30% or more of the peers, then the problem-solving team would consider the role that core instruction plays in student performance first.
2. Determine the current benchmark expectation. For this student the benchmark is 68 words per minute for winter of 2nd grade.
3. Establish the Gap: Divide 68 wpm (the expected benchmark) by 20 wpm (the student's current performance). 68/20 = 3.4. The student's performance is 3.4 times discrepant from that of grade-level peers. The Gap the student has to close by the end of the year is greater than 3.4, since the benchmark will be higher at the end of the year.
4. Determine if the Gap is significant. Any Gap at or greater than 2.0 should be considered significant. For this student, considerable intervention will be needed to close the gap since it is more than 2.0.
5. The next phase of Gap analysis includes determining what constitutes "sufficient progress" that would be necessary to close the Gap. To determine the necessary gain needed to close the Gap, subtract the student's current performance from the expected benchmark in the next benchmark period (i.e., end of the year). For this student the calculation is as follows: 90 wpm (end of year benchmark)—20 wpm (student's current performance) = 70 wpm (necessary to close the gap).
6. At this point, the problem-solving team determines what progress is needed and whether it is realistic for the student. 70 wpm (necessary

gain) divided by 15 (number of weeks for intervention) = 4.6 wpm (weekly gain needed).

The problem-solving team then considers whether this is a realistic goal for the student. If the weekly goal seems unrealistic, the team might change the number of weeks estimated to reach the target based on "reasonable" weekly growth. For example, if a more realistic anticipated gain is 3 words per week, the number of weeks to reach the target would equal 70 (necessary gain) divided by 3 wpm (weekly gain) to establish the anticipated length of intervention as 23 weeks. [It is important to note that the extended number of weeks may result in a slightly higher benchmark/target that would have to be considered.]

The PST Model as a Tool for Diagnosing a Learning Disability

The process begins to require more technical and clinical expertise when students are suspected of having a learning disability (as noted in Chapters 3 and 4). In our PST meetings, it is clear that some students are low in motivation, have poor attendance, or just need a specific, targeted support. For this group, we are not as concerned about goal lines and gap analysis. For students who we suspect may have a learning disability, an additional layer of interventions and progress monitoring is expected according to a formulaic protocol handed down by our state and district. This is when we work closely with our special education department and school psychologist to ensure we are following the letter of the law while doing what is best for students in the process. Parents are involved immediately and provided with frequent updates of progress or concerns.

The research on the matter has produced significant argument. One particular model that is showing promise involves performance and growth rates (CBM and dual discrepancy). The use of dual discrepancy and CBM factors will ask schools to document quality classroom instruction, comparing overall class performance with other classes, districts, PLCs, and so on, and to verify if there is a significant gap (1 standard deviation for CBM with classmates) and difference of 1 standard deviation among growth rates (Gresham, 2007). A consensus is emerging that there should be at least two interventions over a six-week period, and then an eight-week intervention (Gresham, 2007). Although such a model (use of CBM and dual discrepancy) is complex, challenging, and requires major changes for schools, the results are worth the effort (Speece, Case, and Molloy, 2003).

Appendix B

Curriculum-Based Measure (CBM) for Math

1. $-7 + 12 =$

2. $15 - 23 =$

3. $-6(-8) =$

4. $-15 - 19 =$

5. $8 - 4(2 + 6) =$

6. $\dfrac{4 - 13}{3} + 2 =$

7. Solve for v: $4v = -52$
   $v =$

8. Solve for k: $18 = -9 + k$
   $k =$

9. If 1 meter (m) equals 100 centimeters (cm), 9.5 meters is equal to _____ centimeters.

10. Give the next value in the pattern:
    3   19   35   _____

11. $\dfrac{3}{4}(20)$ in simplest form =

12. Evaluate the following expression if $a = 3$:
    $12a - 4a^2 =$

13. Choose the closest estimate for n.

    a) −1.5   c) 1.0
    b) 0.5   d) −0.5

14. Place one of the following symbols between each set of values to make true statements ($<$, $>$, $=$).

    a) 32 _____ 23   c) $\dfrac{6}{8}$ _____ 0.75

    b) 9.605 _____ 9.61

15. Name the coordinates of point A.

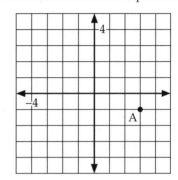

    A = (_____ , _____)

16. Use the grid to graph the point: $(-3,0)$

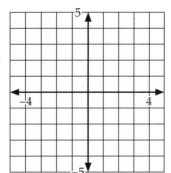

17. Solve for p:

    $$\frac{p}{9} = \frac{4}{6}$$

    $p =$

18. Solve for x:

$$10 = -4 + 2x$$

$x =$

19. Fill in the missing part of the table:

x	y
0	7
1	2
2	−3
3	

20. Fill in the missing part of the table:

x	0	1	2
y	7		6

21. Circle the table that matches the graph:

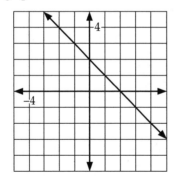

x	y
−1	1
0	2
1	3

x	y
−1	3
0	2
1	1

x	y
−1	0.5
0	1
1	1.5

22. Circle the equation that matches the table:

x	y
−1	1
0	2
1	3

$y = x + 2$ $y = -x - 2$ $y = -2x + 1$

23. Circle the graph that matches the given equation:

$$y = 2x - 1$$

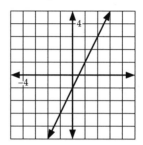

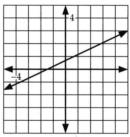

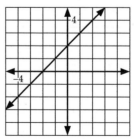

Progress Monitoring (Appendix B continued)

The purpose of progress monitoring should not be to diagnose a disability. The purpose is to gauge how well a student is progressing and the overall effectiveness of instruction, curriculum, and interventions. Based on our own experience, the power of progress monitoring lies in its ability to

1. Highlight student concerns early
2. Give timely feedback to students about performance
3. Evaluate effectiveness of interventions (and model them if they are effective)
4. Highlight curricular concerns regarding the immersion of remediation
5. Provide a body of evidence about a student's response to research-based interventions and quality Tier 1 instruction.

Progress monitoring can be done in a variety of ways. Many resources are available to educators for monitoring student progress, some of which are included in the Resources section of this book. For high schools, the question we must ask of teachers is this: how will you know if students are progressing in the basics or on standards (especially if they are behind)?

For progress monitoring to be effective and meaningful, it should meet the following conditions:

1. It should be timed and brief, lasting less than ten minutes and establishing fluency as one key measure.
2. It should be frequent (the higher the tier, the more frequent), depending on the goals and intensity of needs.
3. It should be rapidly graded for quick feedback.
4. Administration protocol should be common across all classes for uniformity.
5. It should be correlated and aligned with content and pacing. It should be common across PLCs, classrooms, and teachers for the sake of comparison and information-gathering and to avoid the perils of false positive disability diagnosis.
6. It should provide valuable data that can be used for intervention programs; data analysis offers opportunity for response in the classroom.
7. It should use the same or similar set of skills with the same degree of difficulty so progress can be monitored over time, allowing students to track their own data, self-monitor and reflect, and set goals.

8. It should measure one of the key areas of basic skills (math computation, reading comprehension, vocabulary) that aligns with content-area benchmarks (standards-based, ideally) and could indicate the presence of a disability.

This measure of basics is not meant to be a measure of higher-level thinking. Nor is it meant to be a rigorous sample of the entire year's curriculum. We have tried both of those methods, specifically in freshmen algebra, and many others on our pathway to a more efficient progress-monitoring program. The CBM tool above, for example, is instead designed to measure the prerequisite skills (pre-algebraic) that underlie the ability to do algebra with proficiency. Students who struggle with integers or graphing points, for instance, will struggle mightily in a freshman algebra course unless intensive interventions are administered early. That is the primary purpose of this instrument: to identify those students likely to struggle, to remediate the specific difficulty they face in their pre-algebra skills, and then to measure their progress over the course of the school year. The same concept can be applied to other subject areas as well.

Similar versions of the progress-monitoring tool, with the same type of question at each spot and a similar degree of difficulty, are developed to be administered throughout the school year. Our freshman algebra teachers administer this measure every two weeks after the initial screening. This process continues all year, and all students track their own progress on a graph. Team members compare the results across PLC groups to analyze the data and discuss the curricular and pedagogical implications.

The progress monitoring process has been especially helpful in intervention classes and for the student support center. It provides an ideal mechanism by which we can provide remediation support to students without taking away from any instructional time (because we pull them from study hall). Having students track their own progress also puts the responsibility on students to make gains and reach a goal. There are other measures that are similar (AIMSweb now has a pre-algebra probe called MCAP, and Math Mates offers a similar tool). Ultimately, moving from this "skill based" progress monitoring into a more "standards based" monitoring will empower high schools to more effectively chart a student's growth towards proficiency.

Appendix C

Summary of Research-Based Math Strategies

In order to support struggling math students in the classroom, a summary of research findings (from the National Research Center on Learning Disabilities, National Council of Teachers of Mathematics , Principal's Partnership and Center on Instruction) indicates that the following elements and strategies should be in place (though this list is not exhaustive):

- ◆ Blend explicit and open-ended problem-solving opportunities into systematic and strategic instruction
  - Procedural rules, self-regulation (metacognition), cues, memory retention/retrieval and mnemonics: need the rationale behind the strategy in order to activate cognitive and metacognitive processes
  - Small-group instruction is particularly suited for explicit and strategic instruction (more immediate feedback, more chances for practice)
- ◆ Start with the toughest problem first to strengthen problem-solving skills
- ◆ Seek to improve attitudes toward mathematics and motivation
  - Focus on application to real-world problems and implementation of a variety of teaching strategies
  - Encourage writing for reflection and content (journals)
  - Use cooperative groups
  - Establish a community of learners
  - Emphasize constructivist teaching, although discovery learning is insufficient for students with math disabilities: they need mediated instruction
- ◆ Guided use of graphing calculator improves problem-solving skills and increases understanding of math concepts
- ◆ Think-aloud strategies are powerful
  - Law of parsimony
  - Teach a few strategies well
  - Teach students to monitor their own learning and performance
  - Teach when/how/where to use for generalization
  - Integrate strategy instruction into general curriculum
  - Provide ongoing distributed practice and feedback

- Accept that there are limits and difficulties (it can be difficult to modify strategies for SLD students for various situations; not all students benefit)
◆ Peer tutoring (partnering strong students with weak students) and focusing on skills to develop will build persistence in problem-solving
  - Dyads are better than cooperative learning for this process
  - Teach peers how to help each other (prompt cards provided)
  - Provide reciprocal chances
  - Provide data and feedback frequently.

Glossary of Terms and Acronyms

ACT: College Readiness exam and PLAN (earlier years' exam for ACT preparation)

ALEKS: Assessment and Learning in Knowledge Spaces

AP: Advanced Placement

Bx: Behavior incidents

CBM: curriculum-based measures, a simple set of procedures for repeated measurement of student growth toward long-range instructional goals (Deno, 1985)

CSAP: Colorado State Assessment Program, annual standards-based state test for grades 3 through 10.

DBDM: data-based decision-making

ELL: English language learner

G/T: gifted and talented

HSS: High School Success, a guided study hall meant to encourage independent study habits; goal setting, tracking and attainment; content support; and access to SSC for remediation support

IAG: Integrated Algebra Geometry (blended approach to algebra geometry instruction that spreads typical algebra 1, geometry 1, and algebra 2 as a blended model across three years)

IB: International Baccalaureate

IDEA: Individuals with Disabilities Education Act

LRT: literacy resource teacher

MAP: Measure of Academic Progress (benchmarking assessment given by NWEA)

McREL: Mid-continent Research for Education and Learning, the Aurora, Colorado, publisher of Marzano, Gaddy, & Dean's book *What Works in Classroom Instruction* (2000).

NWEA: Northwest Evaluation Association

ODR: office disciplinary referral

PBIS: positive behavior and intervention support

PD: professional development

PLC: professional learning community

PST: problem-solving team

SCM: student-centered meetings

SET: schoolwide evaluation tool

SRI: Scholastic Reading Inventory

SIRF: Screening and Intervention Record Form

SLD: specific learning disability, also referred to as LD

SMART goal: Specific, Measurable, Attainable, Relevant, and Time-bound

SSC: student support center (central intervention location designed to flexibly deliver student support across tiers, across contents, during the school day)

STP: standard treatment protocol (prescribed intervention treatment, often with script and a fixed duration)

Resources

For Parents

www.ncld.org/publications-a-more/parent-advocacy-guides/a-parent-guide-to-rti
www.nrcld.org/resource_kit/parent/What_is_RTI2007.pdf
www.wrightslaw.com/info/rti.parent.guide.htm

General

ACT: www.act.org/news/data.html
Center on Innovation and Improvement: www.centerii.org/
Center on Instruction: www.centeroninstruction.org/
Colorado Department of Education Growth Model: www.schoolview.org/
Colorado Department of Education (CDE) RTI principles: www.cde.state.co.us/RtI/
    SixComponents.htm
Doing What Works: http://dww.ed.gov/
Education Development Center (EDC): www.edc.org/themes/schools
High School Tiered Intervention Initiative (HSTII)—including National High
    School Center, National Center on Response to Intervention, and Center on
    Instruction
Institute for Education Sciences (IES): ies.ed.gov/
Marzano Institute: http://www.marzanoresearch.com/site/
National Center for Research on Evaluation, Standards, and Student Test-
    ing (CRESST): http://lsc-net.terc.edu/do.cfm/resource/8023/show/
    use_set-ow_assess
National Center on Response to Intervention: www.rti4success.org/
National Comprehensive Center for Teacher Quality: www.tqsource.org/
National Dissemination Center for Children with Disabilities: http://www.nichcy
    .org/Pages/Home.aspx
National Education Association: www.nea.org
National Implementation Research Network: www.fpg.unc.edu/~nirn/
    implementation/06/06_stagesimple.cfm
National Institute for Child Health and Development Studies
National Joint Committee on Learning Disabilities
National Reading Panel: http://www.nationalreadingpanel.org/
National Research Center on Learning Disabilities: www.nrcld.org/resources/
National Research Council Panel on Minority Overrepresentation
National Summit on Learning Disabilities: http://www.connectlive.com/events/
    learningsummit/
Palmer High School's website with RtI links and student support center informa-
    tion: http://www.d11.org/palmer/

Presidential Commission on Excellence in Special Education: http://www2.ed
.gov/inits/commissionsboards/whspecialeducation/index.html
RtI Action Network: www.rtinetwork.org/
RtI State Chart Database: http://state.rti4success.org/index.php?option=com_chart
State Implementation & Scaling-up of Evidence-based Practices (SISEP): www.
scalingup.org

Intervention

Florida Center for Reading Research: www.fcrr.org/FCRRReports/index.aspx
Intervention Central: www.interventioncentral.org/
Kansas University, Center for Research on Learning (Strategic Instruction Model):
www.ku-crl.org/sim/
Pre-Referral Intervention Manual by McCarney, S. B., & Wunderlich, K.C., (2006).
Hawthorne Education Services, Columbia, MO.
National Reading Panel: www.nationalreadingpanel.org/Publications/
publications.htm
What Works Clearinghouse: http://ies.ed.gov/ncee/wwc/

Positive Behavior and Intervention Support

OSEP Technical Assistance Center on Positive Behavioral Interventions and Supports (PBIS): www.pbis.org/default.aspx

Professional Learning Communities

Professional Learning Community: http://pdonline.ascd.org/pd_online/
secondary_reading/el200405_dufour.html

Progress monitoring

National Center on Progress Monitoring: www.studentprogress.org/
Research Institute on Progress Monitoring: www.progressmonitoring.org/

Special Education

Council for Exceptional Children: www.cec.sped.org

IDEA Partnership: http://ideapartnership.org/index.php?option=com_content&
view=category&layout=blog&id=15&Itemid=56

IDEA Regulations, Identification of Specific Learning Disabilities: http://idea.ed
.gov/explore/view/p/%2Croot%2Cdynamic%2CTopicalBrief%2C23%2C

Learning Disabilities Association of America (LDA): www.ldaamerica.org/about/
position/print_rti.asp

National Association of School Psychologists: www.nasponline.org/resources

National Dissemination Center for Children with Disabilities: www.nichcy.org/
pages/rti.aspx

OSEP Responsiveness to Intervention in the SLD Determination Process:
www.osepideasthatwork.org/toolkit/pdf/RTI_SLD.pdf

What You Need to Know about IDEA 2004 Response to Intervention (RTI): New
Ways to Identify Specific Learning Disabilities: www.wrightslaw.com/info/rti
.index.htm

Learning Disabilities Roundtable (includes ten separate agencies, as follows):

American Speech-Language-Hearing Association (ASHA): www.asha.org

Association for Higher Education and Disability (AHEAD): www.ahead.org

Council for Exceptional Children, Division for Communicative Disabilities and
Deafness (DCDD): www.gsu.edu/~wwwdhh/

Council for Exceptional Children, Division for Learning Disabilities (DLD):
www.TeachingLD.org

Council for Learning Disabilities (CLD): www.cldinternational.org

International Dyslexia Association (IDA): www.interdys.org/index.jsp

International Reading Association (IRA): www.ira.org/

Learning Disabilities Association of America (LDA): www.ldaamerica.org

National Association of School Psychologists (NASP): www.nasponline.org/
index2.html

National Center for Learning Disabilities (NCLD): www.ld.org

References

Ainsworth, L., Almeida, L., Davies, A., Dufour, R., Gregg, L., Guskey, T., Marzano, R., O'Connor, K., Stiggins, R., White, S., William, D., & Reeves, D. (2007). In D. Reeves (Ed.) *Ahead of the Curve: The Power of Assessment to Transform Teaching and Learning*. Bloomington, IN: Solution Tree Press.

Astuto, T.A., Clark, D. L., Read, A-M., McGree, K., & Fernandez, L.de K. P. (1993). *Challenges to dominant assumptions controlling educational reform*. Andover, MA: Regional Laboratory for the Educational Improvement of the Northeast and Islands.

Bacon, S. (2005). Reading coaches: Adapting an intervention model for upper elementary and middle school readers. *Journal of Adolescent & Adult Literacy, 48*(5), 416–427.

Barnett, D., Daly, E., Jones, K., & Lentz, F. (2004). Response to intervention: Empirically based special service decisions from single-case designs of increasing and decreasing intensity. *Journal of Special Education, 38*, 66–79.

Batsche, G., Elliott, J., Garden, J. L., Grimes, J., Kovaleski, J. F., Prasse, D., Schrag, J., & Tilly, W.D..(2006). Response to intervention: Policy considerations and implementation. Alexandria, VA: National Association of State Directors of Special Education.

Batsche, G., Kavale, K. A., & Kovaleski, J. F. (2006). Competing views: A dialogue on response to intervention. *Assessment for Effective Intervention, 32*, 6–19.

Bender, W. N., & Shores, C. (2007). *Response to intervention: A practical guide for every teacher*. Thousand Oaks, CA: Corwin Press.

Bergan, J. (1977). *Behavioral consultation*. Columbus, OH: Merrill.

Bergan, J., & Kratochwill, T. R. (1990). *Behavioral consultation and therapy*. New York: Plenum Press.

Berkeley, S., Bender, W. N., Peaster, L. G., & Saunders, L. (2009). Implementation of response to intervention: A snapshot of progress. *Journal of Learning Disabilities, 42*, 85–95.

Bransford, J. D. & Stein, B. S. (1993). *The ideal problem solver* (2nd ed.). New York: Freeman.

Brown-Chidsey, R., & Steege, M. (2005). *Response to intervention: Principles and strategies for effective practice*. New York: Guilford Press.

Brozo, W.G. (2010, October). The Role of Content Literacy in an Effective RTI Program. *The Reading Teacher, 64*(2), 147–150.

Burns, M. K., Jacob, S., & Wagner, A. R. (2007). Ethical and legal issues associated with using response to intervention to assess learning disabilities. *Journal of School Psychology, 46*(3), 263–279.

Caplan, G. (1964). *Principles of prevention psychology*. New York: Basic Books.

The Center for Comprehensive School Reform and Improvement. (2008). *Response to intervention: Possibilities for service delivery at the secondary school level*, June Newsletter.

Christenson, S. L., Reschly, A. L., Appleton, J. J., Berman-Young, S., Spanjers, D. M., & Varno, P. (2008). Best practices in fostering student engagement. In A.Thomas & J.Grimes (Eds.), *Best practices in school psychology* (5th ed., pp. 1099–1119). Bethesda, MD: National Association of School Psychologists.

Cobb, B., Sample, P., Alwell, M., & Johns, N. (2005). Effective interventions in dropout prevention: A research synthesis. The effects of cognitive behavioral interventions on dropout prevention for youth with disabilities. Clemson, SC: National Dropout Prevention Center for Students With Disabilities.

Conzemius, A., & O'Neill, J. (2001). Building shared responsibility for student learning. Alexandria, VA: ASCD.

Cortiella, C. (2005). *A parent's guide to response-to-intervention* [Parent Advocacy Brief]. New York: National Center for Learning Disabilities. www.ncld.org/publications-a-more/parent-advocacy-guides/a-parent-guide-to-rti.

Cronbach, L. J. (1975). Beyond two disciplines of scientific psychology. *American Psychologist, 30,* 116–127.

Deno, S. L. (1985). Curriculum-based measurement: The emerging alternative. Exceptional Children, 52, 219- 232

Deno, S. L., Fuchs, L. S., Marston, D., & Shin, J. (2001). Using curriculum-based measurement to establish growth standards for students with learning disabilities. *School Psychology Review, 30,* 507–524.

Deshler, D., & Hughes, C. (2007, April). *RTI and Secondary Schools: How will the game play out?* Invited paper presented at the International Conference for the Council for Exceptional Children, Louisville, KY.

Duffy, H. (2007). *Meeting the needs of significantly struggling learners in high school: A look at approaches to tiered intervention.* Washington, DC: American Institutes for Research, National High School Center.

Dufour, R., & Eaker, R. (1998). *Professional learning communities at work: Best practices for enhancing student achievement.* Bloomington, IN: National Education Services.

Dufour, R., Eaker, R., and Dufour, R. (2005). *On common ground.* Bloomington, IN: National Educational Services.

Duhon, G. J., Noell, G. H., Witt, J. C., Freeland, J. T., Dufrene, B. A., & Gilbertson, D. N. (2004). Identifying academic skill and performance deficits: The experimental analysis of brief assessments of academic skills. *School Psychology Review, 33,* 429–443.

Duncan, A. Elevating the teaching profession. www.neatodayaction.org/2009/12/09/elevating-the-teaching-profession/.

Fisher, D. (2001). "We're moving on up": Creating a schoolwide literacy effort in an urban high school. *Journal of Adolescent & Adult Literacy, 45*(2), 92–101.

Fletcher, J., Lyon, R., Barnes, M., Stuebing, K., Francis, D., Olson, R., Shaywitz, S., & Shaywitz, B. (2002). Classification of learning disabilities: An evidence-based evaluation. In R. Bradley, L. Donaldson, & D. Hallahan (Eds.), *Identification of learning disabilities* (pp. 185–250). Mahway, NJ: Erlbaum.

Flugum, K. R. & Reschly, D. J (1994). Prereferral interventions: Quality indices and outcomes. *Journal of School Psychology, 32,* 1–14.

Foegen, A., Olson, J. R., & Impecoven-Lind, L. (2008). Developing progress monitoring measures for secondary mathematics. *Assessment for Effective Intervention,* 33(4), 240–249.

Fuchs, D., & Deshler, D. (2007). What we need to know about responsiveness to intervention (and shouldn't be afraid to ask). *Learning Disabilities Research & Practice, 22*(2), 129–136.

Fuchs, D., & Fuchs, L. S. (2006). Introduction to response to intervention: What, why, and how valid is it? *Reading Research Quarterly, 41*(1), 93–99.

Fuchs, D., Fuchs, L. S., & Burish, P. (2000). Peer assisted learning strategies: An evidence-based practice to promote reading achievement. *Learning Disabilities Research & Practice, 15*(2), 85–91.

Fuchs, D., Mock, D., Morgan, P. L., & Young, C. L. (2003). Responsiveness-to-intervention: Definitions, evidence, and implications for the learning disabilities construct. *Learning Disabilities Research and Practice, 18*(3), 157–171.

Gee, J.P. (2001). Reading as situated language: A socio-cognitive perspective. *Journal of Adolescent & Adult Literacy, 44*(8), 714–725.

Gerber, M., & Kauffman, J. M. (1981). Peer tutoring in academic settings. In P. S Strain (Ed.), *The utilization of classroom peers as behavior change agents* (pp. 155–188). New York: Plenum Press.

Goodlad, J. I., Mantle-Bromley, C., & Goodlad, S.J. (2004*). Education for everyone: Agenda for education in a democracy*. San Francisco: Jossey-Bass.

Gresham, F. M. (2001). *Responsiveness to intervention: An alternative approach to the identification of learning disabilities*. Paper presented at the Learning Disabilities Summit, Washington, DC.

Gresham, F. M. (2002). Responsiveness to intervention: An alternative approach to the identification of learning disabilities. In R. Bradley, L. Donaldson, & D. Hallahan (Eds.), *Identification of learning disabilities* (pp. 467–519). Mahway, NJ: Erlbaum.

Gresham, F. M. (2007). Evolution of the response-to-intervention concepts: Empirical foundations and recent developments. In S. Jimerson, M. Burns, & A. VanDerHeyden (Eds.), *Handbook of response to intervention: The science and practice of assessment and intervention* (pp. 10–24). New York: Springer Science.

Gresham, F. M., Reschly, D. J., Tilly, W. D., Fletcher, J., Burns, M., Christ, T., Prasse, D., Vanderwood, M., & Shinn, M. (2006). Comprehensive evaluation of learning disabilities: A response to intervention perspective. *The School Psychologist, 59*, 26–30.

Gresham, F. M., & Witt, J. C. (1997). Utility of intelligence tests for treatment planning, classification, and placement decisions: Recent empirical findings and future directions. *School Psychology Quarterly, 12*, 249-267.

Guskey, T., Erkens, C., Ferriter, W.M., Goodwin, M., Heflebower, T., Hierck, T., Jakicic, C., Kramer, S.V., Overlier, J., Rose, A.B., Vagle, N., & Young, A. (2009). In T. Guskey (Ed.), *Teacher as Assessment Leader*. Bloomington, IN: Solution Tree Press.

Hall, S.L. (2008). *Implementing response to intervention: A principal's guide*. Thousand Oaks, CA: Corwin Press.

Hall, T., & Stegila, A. (n.d). Peer mediated instruction and intervention. National Center on Accessing the General Curriculum. www.cast.org/ncac/PeerMediatedInstructionandIntervention2953.cfm.

Heller, K. A., Holtzman, W. H., & Messick S. (Eds.). (1982). *Placing children in special education: A strategy for equity*. Washington, DC: National Academy Press.

High School Tiered Interventions Initiative (HSTII). (2010). *Tiered interventions in high schools: Using preliminary "lessons learned" to guide ongoing discussion.* Washington, DC: American Institutes for Research.

Hord, S. M. (1997). *Professional learning communities: Communities of continuous inquiry and improvement.* Austin, TX: Southwest Educational Development Laboratory.

Jimerson, S. R., Reschly, A. L., & Hess, R. (2008). Best practices in increasing the likelihood of high school completion. In A. Thomas & J.Grimes (Eds.), *Best practices in school psychology* (5th ed., pp. 1085–1097). Bethesda, MD: National Association of School Psychologists.

Johnson, E. S., Mellard, D. F., Fuchs, D., & McKnight, M. A. (2006). *Responsiveness to intervention (RTI): How to do it.* Lawrence, KS: National Research Center on Learning Disabilities.

Johnson, E. S., & Smith, L. (2008). Implementation of response to intervention at middle school: Challenges and potential benefits. *Teaching Exceptional Children, 40*(3), 46–52.

Johnson, E. S., Smith, L., & Harris, M. L. (2009). *How RTI works in secondary schools.* Thousand Oaks, CA: Corwin Press.

Joyce, B., & Showers, B. (1988). *Student achievement through staff development.* White Plains, NY: Longman.

Kavale, K. A. (1990). Effectivness of special education. In T. B. Gutkin & C. R. Reynolds (Eds.), *The Handbook of School Psychology* (pp. 868–898). New York: John Wiley.

Kavale, K. A., Kauffman, A. S., Naglieri, J. A., & Hale, J. (2005). Changing procedures for identifying learning disabilities: The danger of poorly supported ideas. *The School Psychologist, 59*, 15–25.

Kovaleski, J. F. (2003, December). *The three-tier model for identifying learning disabilities: Critical program features and system issues.* Paper presented at the National Research Center on Learning Disabilities Responsiveness-to-Intervention Symposium, Kansas City, MO.

Kovaleski, J. F. (2006). Bringing instructional support teams to scale: Implications of the Pennsylvania experience. *Remedial and Special Education, 27*, 16–25.

Kovaleski, J. F. (2007). Potential pitfalls of response to intervention. In S. Jimerson, M. Burns, & A. VanDerHeyden (Eds.), *Handbook of response to intervention: The science and practice of assessment and intervention* (pp. 80–89). New York: Springer Science.

Kovaleski, J. F., & Glew, M.C. (2006). Bringing instructional support teams to scale: Implications of the Pennsylvania experience. *Remedial and Special Education, 27*(1), 16-25.

Kovaleski, J. F., & Marco, C. M. (2005). *Screening information recording form* (SIRF). Unpublished manuscript.

Kovaleski, J. F., & Pedersen, J. A. (2008). *Best practices in data-analysis teaming.* In A. Thomas and J. Grimes, (Eds.), Best practices in school psychology V (pp.115-129). Bethesda, MD: National Association of School Psychologists.

Kratochwill, T. R., Volpiansky, P., Clements, M., & Ball, C. (2007). Professional development in implementing and sustaining multitier prevention models: Implications for response to intervention. *School Psychology Review, 36*, 618–631.

Kurz, A., Elliot, S. N., Wehby, J. N., & Smithson, J. L. (2009). Alignment of the intended, planned and enacted curriculum in general and special education and its relation to student achievement. *The Journal of Special Education, 43*(3), 1–15.

Learning Disabilities Association of America (LDA). (2006). Response to intervention: Position paper of the Learning Disabilities Association of America. www.ldanatl.org/about/position/rti.asp.

Learning Disabilities Roundtable. (2002, July). *Specific learning disabilities: Finding common ground.* Washington, DC: American Institutes for Research. www.ldanatl.org/legislative/joint_activities/commonground.asp.

Learning Disabilities Roundtable. (2005, February). *Comments and recommendations on regulatory issues under the Individuals with Disabilities Education Improvement Act of 2004, Public Law 108-446.* www.nasponline.org/advocacy/2004LDRoundtableRecsTransmittal.pdf.

Lenz, B. K., Ehren, B. J., & Deshler, D. D. (2005). The content literacy continuum: A school reform framework for improving adolescent literacy for all students. *Teaching Exceptional Children, 37*(6), 60–63.

Marston, D., Muyskens, P., Lau, M., & Canter, A. (2003). Problem-solving model for decision making with high-incidence disabilities: The Minneapolis experience. *Learning Disabilities Research & Practice, 18,* 187–200.

Martinez, S. & Batsche, G. (2008). *Data-Based Decision Making: Academic and Behavioral Applications.* http://sss.usf.edu/resources/topic/ps_rti/index.html.

Marzano, R. J. (2010). *Formative assessment & standards-based grading.* Bloomington, IN: Marzano Research Laboratory.

Marzano, R. J., Gaddy, B. B., & Dean, C. (2000). *What works in classroom instruction.* Aurora, CO: Mid-continent Research for Education and Learning.

Marzano, R. J, Pickering, D., & Pollock, J. (2001). *Classroom instruction that works: Research-based strategies for increasing student achievement.* Alexandria, VA: Association for Supervision & Curriculum Development.

McCarney, S.B. & Wunderlich, K.C. (2006). *Pre-Referral Intervention Manual.* Columbia, MO: Hawthorne Education Services.

McCarthy, S. J., & Moje, E. (2002). Identity matters. *Reading Research Quarterly, 37*(2), 228–238.

Mellard D. (2003). "Understanding Responsiveness to Intervention in Learning Disabilities Determination," Retrievable at http://www.nrcld.org/ publications/papers/mellard.shtml.

Mellard, D. (2004). *Basic principles of the responsiveness-to-intervention approach.* SchwabLearning.org. www.schwablearning.org/articles.asp?r=1056.

Mellard, D., Byrd, S., Johnson, E, Tollefson, J., & Boesche, L. (2004). Foundations and research on identifying model responsiveness-to-intervention sites. *Learning Disabilities Quarterly, 27,* 243–256.

Mellard, D.F., & Johnson, E. J. (2008). *RtI: A practitioner's guide to implementing response to intervention.* Thousand Oaks, CA: Corwin Press.

Naglieri, J. A. (2007). RTI alone is not sufficient for SLD identification: Convention presentation by OSEP director Alexa Posny. *Communiqué, 35,* 52–53.

National Association of State Directors of Special Education. (2005). *Response to intervention: Policy considerations and implementation.* Alexandria, VA: NASDSE.

National Center on Response to Intervention (March 2010). *Essential Components of RTI—A Closer Look at Response to Intervention.* Washington, DC: U.S. Department of Education, Office of Special Education Programs, National Center on Response to Intervention.

National Joint Committee on Learning Disabilities. (2005). *Responsiveness to intervention and learning disabilities* (report).

National Research Center on Learning Disabilities. (2006). Needs assessment. www.eric.ed.gov/ERICWebPortal/custom/portlets/recordDetails/detailmini.jsp?_nfpb=true&_&ERICExtSearch_SearchValue_0=ED496979&ERICExtSearch_SearchType_0=no&accno=ED496979.

National Research Council. (2002). *Executive summary: Disproportionate representation of minority students in special education.* Washington, DC: Author.

Newmann, F. M., Smith, B. A., Allensworth, E., & Bryk, A. S. (2001). Instructional program coherence: What it is and why it should guide school improvement policy. *Educational Evaluation and Policy Analysis, 23*(4), 297–321.

Noell, G. H., & Gansle, K. A. (2006). Assuring the form has substance: Treatment plan implementation as the foundation for assessing response to intervention. *Assessment for Effective Intervention, 52*(1), 32–39.

O'Brien, D. G., Stewart, R., & Moje, E. (1995). Why content literacy is difficult to infuse into the secondary school: Complexities of curriculum, pedagogy and school culture. *Reading Research Quarterly, 30*(3), 442–463.

O'Connor, R. E., Harty, K. R., & Fulmer, D. (2005). Tiers of intervention in kindergarten through third grade. *Journal of Learning Disabilities*, 38(6), 532–538.

Ofiesh, N. (2006). Response to intervention and the identification of specific learning disabilities: Why we need comprehensive evaluations as part of the process. *Psychology in the Schools, 43*(8), 883–888.

Papalewis, R. (2004). Struggling middle school readers: Successful, accelerating intervention. *Reading Improvement, 41*(1), 24.

President's Commission on Excellence in Special Education. (2002). *A new era: Revitalizing special education for children and their families.* Washington, DC: Author.

Reschly, D. J., & Wood-Garnett, S. (2009). *Teacher preparation for response to intervention in middle and high schools.* Washington, DC: Learning Point Associates, National Comprehensive Center on Teacher Quality.

Reschly, D. J., & Ysseldyke, J. E. (2002). Paradigm shift: The past is not the future. In J. Grimes & A. Thomas (Eds.), *Best Practices in School Psychology, 23 (3/4),* 3–20. Bethesda, MD: National Association of School Psychologists.

Reynolds, C. R., & Shaywitz, S. E. (2009). Response to intervention: Prevention and remediation, perhaps. Diagnosis, no. *Child Development Perspectives, 3,* 44–47.

Rosenshine, B. (1997). Advances in research on instruction. In J. W. Lloyd, E. J. Kameanui, and D. Chard (Eds.), *Issues in educating students with disabilities* (pp. 197–221). Mahwah, NJ: Erlbaum.

Schmoker, M. (2002). *Results: The key to continuous school improvement* (2nd ed.). Alexandria, VA: Association for Supervision and Curriculum Development.

Semrud-Clikeman, M. (2005). Neuropsychological aspects for evaluating learning disabilities. *Journal of Learning Disabilities, 38,* 563–568.

Shannon, G. S. (2007). *Nine characteristics of high-performing schools: A research-based resource for schools and districts to assist with improving student learning.* Office of

Superintendent of Public Instruction, Olympia, Washington. www.k12.wa.us/research/pubdocs/ninecharacteristics.pdf.

Shores, C., & Chester, K. (2009). *Using RTI for school improvement: Raising every student's achievement scores.* Thousand Oaks, CA: Corwin Press.

Speece, D. L., Case, L. P., & Molloy, D. E. (2003). Responsiveness to general education instruction as the first gate to learning disabilities identification. *Learning Disabilities Research & Practice, 18,* 147–156.

Stevens, R., & Rosenshine, B. (1981). Advances in research on teaching. *Exceptional Education Quarterly, 2,* 1–9.

Sugai, G. (2004). *Schoolwide positive behavior support in high schools: What will it take?* Paper presented at the Illinois High School Forum of Positive Behavioral Interventions and Supports, Naperville, Illinois.

Telzrow, C., McNamara, K., & Hollinger, C. (2000). Fidelity of problem-solving implementation and relationship to student performance. *School Psychology Review, 29*(3), 443–461.

Tilly, W. D. III (2003). *How many tiers are needed for successful prevention and early intervention?: Heartland AEA 11's evolution from four to three tiers.* Paper presented at the National Research Center on Learning Disabilities Responsiveness-to-Intervention Symposium, Kansas City, MO.

VanDerHeyden, Witt, and Naquin, 2003. The development and validation of a process for screening referrals to special education. *School Psychology Review, 32,* 204–227.

VanDerHeyden, A. M., Witt, J. C., & Gilbertson, D. (2007). A multi-year evaluation of the effects of a response to intervention (RTI) model on identification of children for special education. *Journal of School Psychology, 45,* 225–256.

Vaughn, S., & Fuchs, L. S. (Eds.). (2003). Special issue: Response to intervention. *Learning Disabilities Research & Practice, 18*(3).

Vaughn, S., & Fuchs, L. S (2003). Redefining learning disabilities as inadequate response to instruction: The promise and potential problems. *Learning Disabilities Research & Practice, 18*(3), 137–146.

Vaughn, S., Wanzek, J., & Fletcher, J. M. (2007). Multiple tiers of intervention: A framework for prevention and identification of students with reading/learning disabilities. In B. M. Taylor & J. Ysseldyke (Eds.), *Educational interventions for struggling readers* (pp. 173–196). New York: Teacher's College Press.

Vogel, Carl. Algebra: Changing the equation. District Administration. www.districtadministration.com/viewarticle.aspx?articleid=1581.

Wiggins, G., and McTighe, J. (2005). *Understanding by design.* Alexandria, VA: Association for Supervision and Curriculum Development.

Windram, H., Scierka, B., & Silberglitt, B. (2007). Response to intervention at the secondary level: Two districts' models of implementation. NASP *Communiqué, 35*(5), from http://www.nasponline.org/publications/cq/mocq355rtisecondary.aspx

Wright, Jim. (2007). *RTI toolkit: A practical guide for schools.* Port Chester, NY: Dude.

Ysseldyke, J., & Marston, D. (1999). Origins of categorical special education services in schools and a rationale for changing them. In D. Reschly, W. D. Tily III, & J. Grimes (Eds.), *Special education in transition: Functional assessment and noncategorical programming* (pp. 1–18). Longmont, CO: Sopris West.